FINDING THE WILD WEST:

ALONG THE MISSISSIPPI

FINDING THE WILD WEST: ALONG THE MISSISSIPPI

LOUISIANA, ARKANSAS, MISSOURI, IOWA, AND MINNESOTA

MIKE COX

TWODOT®

ESSEX, CONNECTICUT
HELENA, MONTANA

A · TWODOT® · BOOK

An imprint and registered trademark of Globe Pequot, the trade division of
The Rowman & Littlefield Publishing Group, Inc.
4501 Forbes Blvd., Ste. 200
Lanham, MD 20706
www.rowman.com

Distributed by NATIONAL BOOK NETWORK

British Library Cataloguing in Publication Information available

Library of Congress Cataloging-in-Publication Data available

ISBN 978-1-4930-6411-3 (paper : alk. paper)
ISBN 978-1-4930-6412-0 (electronic)

♾™ The paper used in this publication meets the minimum requirements of American
National Standard for Information Sciences—Permanence of Paper for Printed Library
Materials, ANSI/NISO Z39.48-1992.

Writers typically dedicate their books to a particular person, but this book is dedicated to a singularly spiritual moment in the once Wild West and the three people who shared it with me. On June 20, 2016, on our way to the annual Western Writers of America conference, Beverly Waak and I, along with our friends Preston and Harriet Lewis, visited the Little Bighorn Battlefield National Monument. In this historic place where two cultures collided so violently, what we perceived, lingering over the still-remote landscape like traces of gun smoke, was an overwhelming sense of peace. At the circular memorial commissioned by the Lakota to honor their fallen warriors, I happened to look up into a dark blue Montana sky. Having traveled to a lot of places over many decades, I had never seen anything like this: a long, high, thin cloud that looked very much like a giant eagle feather. Beverly, Harriet, and Preston saw it too. Freak of weather? Somehow, it didn't feel like that. Rather, it was as if the sky, in concert with the wind and the sun, wanted to remind us with its rendering of such a sacred American Indian icon that no matter what, all of us are connected—to each other, to the past, and to the land.

—Mike Cox

CONTENTS

Minnesota

PREFACE: FINDING THE WILD WEST

Ain't nothing better than riding a fine horse in a new country.
—GUS MCCREA IN *LONESOME DOVE*

LIKE MOST BABY BOOMERS, I LEARNED ABOUT THE OLD WEST IN the mid-1950s and early 1960s watching black-and-white television westerns and John Wayne movies in color. But that was Hollywood's Old West.

Thanks largely to my late granddad, L.A. Wilke, I began to learn about the real Old West. He was born in Central Texas in the fading days of that era, just long enough ago to have learned how to ride a horse well before he ever got behind the wheel of an automobile. Too, as a youngster and later as a newspaperman, he met some notable Wild West figures, from Buffalo Bill Cody to old Texas Rangers who had fought Comanches. A fine storyteller, he shared his experiences with me. Also, he passed his copies of *True West* and *Frontier Times* on to me. At the time, his friend Joe Small published both magazines in Austin, where I grew up.

Even before I started reading nonfiction Western magazines and books, again thanks to Granddad, I got to visit some Old West historic sites when they were still just abandoned ruins. With him, as a first grader I prowled around old Fort Davis in West Texas well before the federal government stabilized it as a National Historic Site. Later, Granddad took me to several southwest New Mexico ghost towns, including Shakespeare, Hillsboro, and Kingston. This was in 1964, when many of that state's roadways were not yet paved. In that desert high country, I experienced for the first time the still-vast openness of the West and the sense of adventure in exploring an old place new to me.

So why was the West wild?

I think you will come to understand the "why" when you experience the "where" of the Wild West. Though many of the sites described in these books are in populated areas, some are as remote or more remote than they were back in the Wild West's heyday. In visiting these sites, say a ghost town well off the beaten path, you should be able to feel the reason why the West was wild. When I stand in the middle of nowhere, distant from nothing, I feel the sense of freedom that must have driven so much of human behavior in frontier times. In such emptiness, usually scenic, it's easy to believe you can do anything you, by God, want to, be it bad or good.

Some see the West as being all the states west of the Mississippi, which includes twenty-three states. Others maintain that the West begins at the ninety-eighth meridian. My belief is that the Mississippi River is what separates the East from the West in the US.

Accordingly, moving from east to west, this series of travel guides divides the West into five regions: along the Mississippi (Louisiana, Arkansas, Iowa, Minnesota, and Missouri); the Great Plains (Oklahoma, Kansas, Nebraska, South Dakota, and North Dakota); the Southwest (Arizona, New Mexico, and Texas); the Mountain West (Colorado, Montana, Nevada, Utah, and Wyoming); and the Pacific West (Alaska, California, Idaho, Oregon, and Washington).

Having described what I consider the West, what constitutes "wild?"

Former Wild West History Association president Robert G. (Bob) McCubbin, a history buff who acquired one of the world's most inclusive collections of Western photographs, ephemera, books, and artifacts, a few years back offered his take on the matter.

"The Wild West was a time and place unique in the history of the world," he wrote. "It took place on the plains, prairies, mountains, and deserts of the American West, from the Mississippi River to the Pacific Ocean. It began about the time of the California gold rush and was at its height in the 1870s through the 1890s, fading away in the decade after the turn of the twentieth century—as the automobile replaced the horse."

He went on to explain that Wild West does not mean wilderness wild. It means lawless wild. While untamed grandeur was certainly a part of the Wild West, it was the untamed men and women who made the West wild.

"Of course," McCubbin continued, "during the Wild West period there were many good and substantial citizens who went about their business in a law abiding and constructive way. Most of those are forgotten. It's the excitement of the Wild West's bad men, desperadoes, outlaws, gunfighters, and lawmen—many of whom were also, at times, cowboys, scouts, and buffalo hunters—and the dance hall girls and 'shady ladies,' who capture our interest and imagination."

While mostly adhering to McCubbin's definition of the Wild West, I could not stick to it entirely. Some things that happened prior to the California gold rush—Spanish and French colonial efforts, the Louisiana Purchase, the Lewis and Clark Expedition, the exploits of mountain men, the development of the great western trails, and the Mexican War of 1846 to 1848—were critical in shaping the later history of the West. That explains why some of the sites associated with these aspects of history needed to be included in this book.

For the most part, 1900 is the cut-off date for events related in this series of books. But the Wild West did not end at 11:59 p.m. on December 31, 1899. Some places, particularly Arizona, Oklahoma, New Mexico, and far west Texas, stayed wild until World War I. Sometimes, events that occurred in the nineteenth century continued to have ramifications in the early twentieth century. An example would be the life and times of Pat Garrett, who killed Billy the Kid in 1881. Garrett himself was shot to death in 1909, so his death site is listed.

The Finding the Wild West series is not intended as a guide to every single historic site in a given city, state, or region. Some towns and cities had to be left out. It would take an encyclopedic, multivolume work to cover *all* the historical places throughout the western states. I have tried to include the major sites with a Wild West connection, along with some places with great stories you've probably never heard.

These books focus primarily on locations where there is still something to see today. Those sites range from period buildings and ruins to battlefields, historical markers, tombstones, and public art. In addition to historic sites, I have included museums and libraries with collections centered on "those thrilling days of yesteryear." Again, I have *not* listed every museum or every attraction.

A note on directions: Since almost everyone has access to GPS applications or devices, locations are limited to specific addresses with "turn here" or "until you come to" used only when necessary, with the exception of block-row-plot numbers of graves (when available). GPS coordinates are given for more difficult to find locations.

The Wild West has long since been tamed, with nationally franchised fast-food places and big-box stores standing where the buffalo roamed and the deer and the antelope played. Considered another way, however, the Wild West hasn't gone anywhere. It still exists in our collective imagination—a mixture of truth and legend set against the backdrop of one of the world's most spectacular landscapes.

Wild Bill Hickok, Jesse James, George Armstrong Custer, Billy the Kid, Wyatt Earp, and others received a lot of press and rose from the dead as Western icons, but there were many more characters—from outlaws to lawmen, drovers to cattle barons, harlots to preachers—whose stories are yet to be brought to life. Indeed, every tombstone, every historical marker, every monument, every ghost town, every historic site, every place name, every structure, every person has a story to tell. Like a modern-day prospector, all you need to do is pack these books in your saddlebag, mount up, and ride out in search of the Wild West.

—Mike Cox
Wimberley, Texas

INTRODUCTION: ALONG THE MISSISSIPPI

LOUISIANA, ARKANSAS, MISSOURI, IOWA, AND MINNESOTA ALL HAVE differing geography, history, and culture, but they also have one thing in common—they lie along the western bank of the Mississippi River.

Beginning at Lake Itasca in Minnesota, the nation's greatest river flows nearly due south for 2,340 miles before emptying into the Gulf of Mexico. Along the way it is fed by four other large river systems, the Ohio, the Missouri, the Tennessee, and the Red, along with hundreds of smaller streams. While the Mississippi does not cut through the exact geographic center of the nation, it divides the US into its two primary sociopolitical selves, the East and the West.

For much of American history, the long river was more than a blue line on the map. Until supplanted by the development of the nation's railroad system, the Mississippi and its tributaries formed a major transportation artery plied by canoes, keelboats, and flatbottom boats, followed later by the marvels of the mid-nineteenth century— paddle wheel steamboats. On the other hand, the river constituted a formidable barrier. Wide and often treacherous, it and its major tributaries were not easy bodies of waters to cross. But to settle the West, that had to be done.

The US acquired the land it later divided into the five states along the west side of the river—and much more—as part of the Louisiana Purchase in 1803. Bought from France for $15 million, the sprawling real estate acquisition doubled the size of the nation, extending it from the Mississippi to the Rocky Mountains.

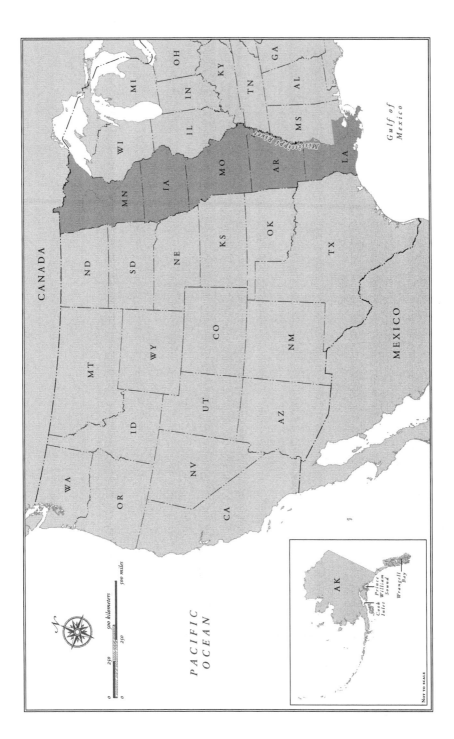

Of the five states that would develop along the Mississippi, Louisiana was the first admitted to the union. When that happened in 1812, the rest of the land purchased by President Thomas Jefferson was renamed Missouri Territory to avoid confusion with the new state of Louisiana.

Carved from the southeastern corner of that territory, Missouri became the twenty-fourth state in 1821. At roughly the mid-point of the river, it evolved as the principal gateway to the West and the starting point of the Santa Fe, Oregon, and California Trails as well as the Pony Express and the Butterfield Overland Mail.

Congress had designated roughly the bottom fifth of Missouri Territory, an area stretching from the Mississippi on the east to the Red River on the west as Arkansas Territory in 1819. The eastern half of this territory became the state of Arkansas in 1836 while the western half eventually became Oklahoma.

Iowa was made a territory in 1833 and a state in 1846, followed by Minnesota, which gained territorial status in 1849 and became the thirty-eighth state of the union in 1858.

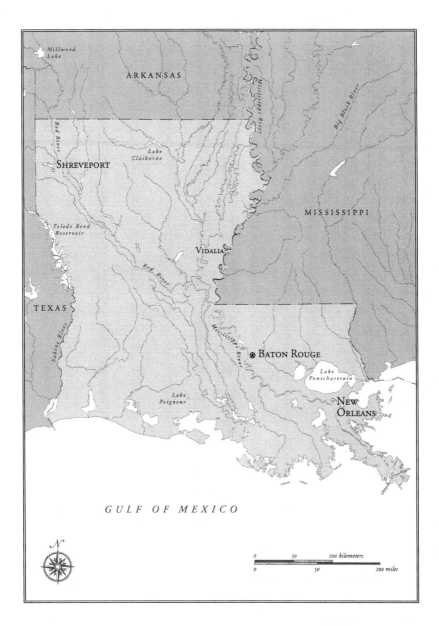

LOUISIANA

ALEXANDRIA (RAPIDES PARISH)

Alexandria developed from a French trading post on the Red River called *Post du Rapides* because of the rapids on that segment of the river. Alexander Fulton, possessing a Spanish land grant, began locating settlers in the area in the late 1700s. In 1805, he and a business partner surveyed a townsite they named in Fulton's honor. Alexandria was incorporated in 1818 and grew as an agricultural supply center.

In 1837 it became the first city west of the Mississippi River with a railroad connection when cotton grower and engineer Ralph Smith laid sixteen miles of track from his land to the wharves at Alexandria. By the time the Civil War broke out, the line extended to near Cheneyville, a distance of forty miles. Once the city recovered from the war, it again flourished as a timber shipping point and rail center.

The **Louisiana Museum of History** (503 Washington St.; 318-487-8557) is housed in the former public library, built in 1907. Founded in 1867, the **Alexandria National Cemetery** (209 East Shamrock, Pineville) has more than ten thousand military burials, including unidentified remains reburied there following their removal from abandoned western forts, including Forts Brown and Ringgold in Texas. Some of the reburials from Fort Brown, in the lower Rio Grande valley, were of soldiers killed in the early stage of the 1846–1848 Mexican War.

ATLANTA (WINN PARISH)

One of Louisiana's most notorious Wild West characters was, ironically enough, a man named West—**John R. West** (1830–1870).

West fought for the South during the Civil War until he was captured on July 4, 1863, when Union forces finally prevailed in their siege of Vicksburg, Mississippi. Paroled during Reconstruction on the promise that he would no longer bear arms against federal troops, West began bearing arms against hapless travelers on the Harrisonburg Road, which intersected the heavily traveled road from Natchez, Mississippi, to San Antonio in Texas. Of course West and his principal cohort, **Lawson "Laws" Kimbrell** represented themselves and their followers as citizens' home guards dedicated to maintaining law and order. And by day they conducted themselves as respected members of the community. But when the sun went down, vampire-like they reverted to highwaymen, robbing and killing. They were known variously as the West-Kimbrell Clan or the Nightriders.

All went well for them and bad for many travelers (whose bodies they often dumped in wells) until Easter Sunday 1870. On one of the holiest days of the year for Christians, a group of concerned Winn Parish residents executed West and four of his fellow gang members by firing squad. Kimbrell, the *New Orleans Times* reported on May 2, "was shot down for dead, but the ball only scalped him, and he made his escape." Within three years, however, Kimbrell was hanged for robbery and murder on April 14, 1873, in Austin, Texas.

West is buried in **Atlanta Cemetery** (just northeast of the intersection of Main Street and School Road).

In 2018, at the intersection of US 167 and State Highway 500 in Packton, on the boundary between Winn and Grant Parishes, the Grant Parish Preservation Board and the Grant Parish Planning Commission erected a metal marker summarizing the West-Kimbrell story.

One of the gang's better-known robbery victims, Simeon G. Butts, a former Union army lieutenant killed on July 9, 1866, is buried beneath a simple, ground-level marker in **Yankee Springs Cemetery** (760 Yankee Springs Rd., Winn Parish).

Baton Rouge (East Baton Rouge Parish)

In 1699 a French explorer came to an Indian village on the Mississippi upriver from future New Orleans and noticed an unusual object, a tall cypress pole stained red with animal blood. Hanging from it were dried fish heads and an assortment of bleached bear bones. The pole, the visitor learned from friendly natives, marked the boundary separating the hunting grounds of the Houma and Bayogoulas Indians.

In French, "the red pole" (or "stick") is *le baton rouge,* and that's how Baton Rouge got its name.

Settled in 1719, Baton Rouge grew to become a busy port city, the capital of Louisiana, and a place with a rich history covering more than three hundred years.

In 1819, Louisiana having been acquired by the US sixteen years earlier, the army established a fortified supply depot that continued to grow, in size and strategic importance. During the Mexican War it was an important staging area as troops moved into the former Republic of Texas on their way to the Rio Grande and beyond. After the US military abandoned the post, the Louisiana state militia occupied it. During the Civil War, it was used by the Confederacy and later occupied by federal troops during the Battle of Baton Rouge.

Built in 1838 and listed on the National Register of Historic Places, the **Old Arsenal Museum** (900 State Capitol Dr.; 225-219-3700) is located on the grounds of the new statehouse. Considered perhaps the most historic place in Baton Rouge, the arsenal served as the powder magazine for the nearby army post. At the time, the installation was one of the most strategically important garrisons west of the Mississippi. Exhibits in the museum focus on the city and state's military history and the Civil War. Some graffiti dating from this period can still be seen carved in the old magazine's walls.

When Baton Rouge became the state capital (New Orleans was Louisiana's first capital), the government constructed a Gothic, castle-like statehouse overlooking the Mississippi. Surviving fires, a war, and numerous renovations, the building continued in use until the present capital was built in the 1930s. Mark Twain was not an admirer of the 1849 building. Referring to it as "this little sham castle," he blamed its design on Sir Walter Scott, saying it would not have been built if the Scottish novelist "had not run the people mad . . . with his medieval romances." Today **Louisiana's Old State Capitol** (100 North Blvd.; 225-342-0500) houses a state museum focused on the state's political history.

The **Capitol Park Museum** (660 North 4th St.; 225-342-5428) provides an overview of Louisiana's history.

The **LSU Rural Life Museum** (4560 Essen Ln.; 225-765-2437) documents what life was like outside Louisiana's towns and cities with restored eighteenth- and nineteenth-century structures, artifacts, and exhibits. Opened in 1970 and managed by the Louisiana State University Agricultural Center, the museum is located on an old plantation.

FRANKLINTON (WASHINGTON PARISH)

Sixty-one miles north of New Orleans, Franklinton was founded as Franklin in 1819 and became the seat of Washington Parish in 1821. The "ton" was added to the name in 1826 because there was another town in Louisiana called Franklin.

One of the Wild West's more noted train robbers, **Eugene Bunch** (1843–1892), lived with his family in the Franklinton area and that's where he died. But his demise was not attributable to old age.

Bunch grew up in a good family, fought for the South during the Civil War, and was well-educated for the times. In the early 1870s he moved to Texas, near the Red River north of Dallas–Fort Worth, where he was later elected county clerk of Cooke County. He taught school for a time and later edited a newspaper in Wichita Falls, Texas. But by 1881, he transitioned from heavy drinking and gambling to committing major felonies, specifically armed train robberies.

Though they suspected Bunch of several robberies in Texas, including a holdup of a Southern Pacific train east of El Paso, local, state, and federal officers were unable to make a case against him. He left Texas in 1888 and returned to Louisiana, where he continued robbing trains. Most of the time, he did so single-handedly.

When he robbed an Illinois Central train north of Franklinton in April 1892—this time with a partner—the railroad hired private detective Thomas V. Jackson to find the outlaw. With the help of an informant who ended up getting murdered, Jackson and a posse encountered Bunch and a fellow outlaw in a thickly wooded area of Washington Parish on August 21, 1892. The lesser criminal was taken into custody, but Bunch's bullet-riddled body soon lay on display in

Franklinton. Bunch was later buried in **Morris Cemetery** off South Main Street (Highway 16).

The **D. A. Varnado Store Museum** (936 Pearl St.; 985-795-0680) focuses on local history.

HOMER (CLAIBORNE PARISH)

When the Claiborne Parish courthouse in Athens burned in the fall of 1849, the parish government decided that the next courthouse should be more centrally located. That was the beginning of another town with a classics-inspired name, Homer.

Incorporated in 1850, the community grew rapidly and Claiborne Parish—its economy based on cotton growing—became one of the more prosperous political subdivisions in the state. One of the many people attracted to the area was one **John Lumpkin Garrett** (1822–1868), who around 1853 arrived from Alabama with his wife Elizabeth Ann Jarvis (1829–1867) and their children, including three-year-old **Patrick Floyd Garrett**. The elder Garrett acquired a mid-size plantation and became a prosperous cotton grower.

Completed in 1861 at a cost of $12,304.36, the two-story Greek revival **Claiborne Parish Courthouse** is said to have been designed by John Garrett and built with enslaved labor from Garrett's plantation. The structure is one of only four surviving antebellum courthouses in Louisiana and the only one still serving as the seat of parish government.

Enslaved people toiled in Garrett's fields, but when his son was old enough, John put Pat to work as a clerk in the plantation store. When he wasn't working or going to school, the boy hunted squirrels and rabbits and learned to shoot well. The Civil War, in which Pat was too young and his father not healthy enough to fight, left the family impoverished. But that didn't subdue John Garrett's Southern sympathies. During Reconstruction, he gunned down a Unionist on the courthouse steps. The man survived and no charges were filed.

Mrs. Garrett died in 1867, followed by her husband a year later. The estate became tangled in legal matters, and Pat threatened to kill the administrator, no matter that it was his brother-in-law. Garrett managed to keep his anger in check, but he must have realized there was nothing left for him in Louisiana. In 1869 the tall, lanky teenager headed to Texas. Within a dozen years, as sheriff of Lincoln County in New Mexico Territory, Pat Garrett would achieve Wild West immortality by killing an outlaw named Billy the Kid.

A historical marker dedicated in 2019 detailing Garrett's time in northwest Louisiana is located at the public library (909 Edgewood Dr.) in Homer.

John and Elizabeth Garrett are buried just inside the gate of the **Old Homer Cemetery** (West 3rd and North 5th Streets).

LOGANSPORT (DESOTO PARISH)

Injury, childbirth, and disease know no borders and neither did **Dr. Richard Logan**, who in 1830 built a ferry to carry settlers across the Sabine River from Louisiana into Texas. That way, he could treat patients on either side of the river. The settlement at this point on the Sabine originally was known as Waterloo, but because of the ferry, people started calling it Logan's Ferry and finally, when a post office was established there, Logansport.

On the Louisiana side of the Texas-Louisiana border is a ten-foot, nine-inch-square piece of granite sunk into the ground on April 23, 1841, to mark the survey line separating the US from what was then the Republic of Texas. It is one of only two surviving international boundary markers known to exist in the continental US. Listed on the National Register of Historic Places, the marker along with two modern historical markers stands in a three-acre roadside park north of Logansport near the junction of Louisiana Highway 765 and Texas Farm to Market Road 31.

Despite its status as a waypoint for Texas-bound travelers, the town did not see significant growth until a rail line opened in 1884 connecting Houston, Texas, with Shreveport. After that, for a time Logansport was a rough town with more saloons than grocery stores.

The Story Moses Rose Told

In 1842 a fifty-something Frenchman—a veteran of Napoleon's army—moved to Logansport from Natchitoches. Before arriving in Louisiana, he had lived in the old East Texas town of Nacogdoches. His name was **Louis "Moses" Rose**.

In Logansport, he became friends with Aaron Ferguson, a Desoto Parish plantation owner and veteran of the War of 1812. Ferguson provided Rose a place to stay, but for his kindness the planter was rewarded with a fair amount of trouble. As Rose grew older, he became increasingly weaker, bed-ridden by chronic sores on his legs and other health issues. He died in 1851 at around sixty-five years old.

Rose's name would have amounted to nothing more than a bit of engraving on a tombstone except for one thing: He may have been the only man to escape from the Alamo. It is his account of his last day in the besieged San Antonio mission that gave rise to one of the world's more enduring metaphors: "The line in the sand."

Rose told his story to the pioneer couple who took him in when he staggered up to their East Texas cabin in the late spring of 1836 after walking some two hundred miles from San Antonio. However, thirty-seven years passed before their son, William Zuber, related the episode in the 1873 edition of the *Texas Almanac*. In his article, Zuber said that, according to Rose, on March 3, 1836, Alamo commander William Barrett Travis gathered all his men, drew a line on the ground with his saber, and asked all who were prepared to die defending the Alamo to cross the line. Everyone moved to the other side except Rose. Later that night, Zuber wrote, Rose slipped out of the Alamo and managed to make his way to Grimes County in East Texas. In fleeing the besieged fortification, Rose had to run through thick cactus, causing his legs to soon bristle with cactus needles.

Historians continue to debate the veracity of Rose's story, though there is no doubt he participated in Texas's revolution against Mexico. Whatever the truth of his past, Rose is buried in the small **Ferguson Cemetery** (four miles east of Funston, off Highway 168; GPS coordinates: N32° 02.12', W93° 55.99'). A modern gray monument inscribed "Moses Rose 1785–1850 'Soldier of The Alamo'" stands above his grave.

MARKSVILLE (AVOYELLES PARISH)

Most towns are the result of someone's intention, but not Marksville. In 1794, during the time Louisiana was part of the vast Spanish empire, an itinerate Jewish trader named Marco (there are at least three versions of his surname) was traveling through the area when a wagon wheel broke. Not easily able to move on, Marco established a trading post in the vicinity and the settlement that grew around it became known as Marksville.

Predating Marco in the area were members of the **Tunica-Biloxi Tribe**. The early interaction of these American Indians with the Spanish and French is represented in one of the West's more unusual museums. The **Tunica-Biloxi Museum** (150 Melacon Rd.; 218-253-9767) displays a large collection of repatriated European-made trade items and other artifacts left as grave goods by the Tunica-Biloxi people. Managed by the tribe, the museum is located in its forty-thousand-square-foot cultural and educational resources center. The collection—once known as the "Tunica Treasure"—was returned to the tribe from the Peabody Museum of Archeology and Ethnology at Harvard University in accordance with the federal Native American Graves Protection and Repatriation Act of 1990.

Also in Marksville is one of the trans-Mississippi's oldest residences, the **Hypolite Bordelon House** (242 Tunica Dr. West; 318-253-0284). Built around 1820 by one of the area's pioneer families, the house was listed on the National Register of Historic Places in 1980.

MERRYVILLE (BEAUREGARD PARISH)

Only four miles east of the Sabine River, for years Merryville was as much a Texas town as a Louisiana community. The community began as a logging settlement, with timber harvested in the area floated down the Sabine to sawmills in Texas. The arrival of the Jasper and Eastern Railroad in 1909 made it easier to ship timber from there and the town flourished, becoming incorporated in 1912. When most of the land in the area had been clear cut, the town's heyday was over.

"Leather Britches" Smith

Not long after the railroad reached Merryville, so did a hired gunman who was one of the last of the Wild West's gunslingers—**Charles "Leather Britches" Smith**. Of course, few believe that "Charles Smith" was his real name. Some said he was really a man named Bill Myatt.

Whatever his legal identity, no one disputed that he came from Texas, that he was good with a gun, or that he had killed from one to two or more people west of the Sabine. Some said he had tortured and killed his second wife. Others said he'd killed a couple of men in Corsicana, Texas. Or was it in Clarksville on the Red River? Accounts vary.

Some sources say Myatt-Smith (whatever his name) got his nickname because he favored wearing buckskin pants, other accounts have the name coming because his pants were always so dirty and greasy they looked like leather. In Merryville and surrounding small timber industry communities, he carried a pair of .45 revolvers and generally walked around town toting a .30-30 Winchester as well. In modern language, he was a hired goon for a union seeking to represent sawmill workers.

In what became known as the **Grabow Riot**, on July 7, 1912, a shootout erupted between union organizers supporting the Brotherhood of Timber Workers and sawmill security personnel, aka union busters. When the shooting ended, four men lay dead and another fifty had been wounded. Some three hundred shots had been fired.

On September 25, incensed over Myatt-Smith's role in the Grabow incident, a group of concerned citizens gunned him down. For several days, his ice-packed open casket was on display outside the town's small jail.

Leather Britches was buried in the **Merryville Cemetery** (just east of the intersection of Margo Street and State Highway 110). A homemade grave marker simply notes, "Smith, Leather Britches, Slain—1912." But Leather Britches may or may not lie beneath it. Some old-timers later recalled that the gunslinger was so unpopular that he was buried facedown along the graveyard's fence line so as not to pollute the remains of decent folks.

The ruins of the **old poured-concrete jail**, with walls six inches thick, stand just off State Highway 110 at Hennigan Street. The abandoned lockup is on private property, but easily visible from the roadway.

In 2019, a metal marker relating the Leather Britches story was erected on the grounds of the **Merryville Historical Society Museum** (628 North Railroad Ave.; 979-864-0219 or 337-825-6289). The first of a planned series of Louisiana legend and lore markers, it was funded by the William G. Pomeroy Foundation and erected by the Louisiana State University at Lafayette's Center for Louisiana Studies. The museum tells the story of the town and its most famous outlaw.

Adjacent to the museum is the **1882 log cabin** once home to deputy US Marshal Andrew Jackson Burk who served from 1890 until he died two years later in a hunting accident.

Natchitoches (Natchitoches Parish)

The first thing to know about Natchitoches is that it is not pronounced like it looks. The correct way to say it is NAK-a-tish. The second thing to know about this town is that it is the oldest non-Indian settlement in any of the states on land originally part of the Louisiana Purchase.

Founded in 1714 as a French trading post, Natchitoches was later controlled for a time by Spain and then again by France before it became part of American territory in 1803. The town lay astride El Camino Real, a road that connected it with San Antonio, Texas (known as Bexar during Spanish colonial times), and continued all the way to Mexico City. Natchitoches later flourished as a steamboat landing until the Red River changed course in 1825 and left the town high and dry. Still, thanks to the old Spanish road, it continued as a waypoint for Texas-bound travelers, including David Crockett, Sam Houston, and other figures of the Texas Revolution as well as immigrants.

All this history is interpreted at Natchitoches' **Northwest Louisiana History Museum** (800 Front St.; 318-357-2492). In the strange bed fellow category, the Louisiana State Museum system in 2013 opened an architecturally striking $23 million facility as the new home of two previously separate Natchitoches museums—the Courthouse Museum and the Louisiana Sports Hall of Fame. While the latter retained its name and focus, the former was renamed the Northwest Louisiana History Museum as its scope expanded from local to regional. Located adjacent to the sports hall of fame, the museum covers four centuries of northwestern Louisiana history. As the state's website points out, the museum "tells the story of how diverse groups of people—Caddo Indians, French and Spanish settlers, free and enslaved Africans, and rural southern whites—created the region's distinctive culture."

Three significant historic sites lie within a twenty-five-mile radius of Natchitoches: Fort St. Jean Baptiste des Natchitoches, Los Adaes, and Fort Jesup.

A detachment of French marines established Fort St. Jean Baptiste in 1716 to protect the newly opened Natchitoches trading post. When Spain took possession of Louisiana in 1763, the Spanish military briefly maintained a garrison at the fort, but by the time of the Louisiana Purchase the post had fallen to ruin. The original site was lost when the Red River changed course, but the log fort was reconstructed by the state of Louisiana near the original location and the **Fort St. Jean Baptiste Historic Site** (155 Rue Jefferson; 318-357-3101) was created.

Hoping to prevent the French from expanding into East Texas, in 1717 Spain established Mission San Miguel de Linares de los Adaes only fifteen miles west of Natchitoches. Two years later, when war broke out between France and Spain, French soldiers took control of the mission. When the two empires negotiated a truce in 1721, Spain reoccupied Los Adaes and hoped to grow it into a permanent settlement. To that end, it was designated as the capital of the Spanish province of Texas in 1729, a status it held until San Antonio became capital in 1770. Within a few years, Los Adaes withered, and the surrounding pine trees reclaimed the site. Archeologically rich, it remained under private ownership until Natchitoches Parish bought the property in 1931. Having preserved the site, the parish conveyed it to the state in 1979. Today it is maintained as the **Los Adaes State Historic Site** (6354 Highway 485, Robeline; 318-472-9449).

As good as the Louisiana Purchase was for the US, the treaty that stipulated the terms of the sale was not clear as to what constituted the boundary between formerly French Louisiana and Spain, which still held the province of Texas and much of the rest of the Southwest. Spain claimed western Louisiana. The US asserted that it owned all of Louisiana. For the time being, the two nations agreed to disagree on the matter. The result was a large piece of real estate that came to be known as the **Neutral Ground**. The problem was not resolved until 1819, when Congress ratified the Florida Purchase Treaty. That document set the boundary between the US and Spain as the Sabine River.

Prior to this resolution, the Neutral Ground had been a No Man's Land of the first order. It wasn't that no man lived there, but most of those who did were not good men. Outlawry thrived in the area, and travelers on the road to Texas were easy pickings.

But after the US gained control of all of Louisiana, it located an army post in the area in 1822. Established by Lt. Col. Zachary Taylor, the fort was named for Taylor's military patron, Brig. Gen. Thomas Jesup.

Soldiers from the fort protected travelers and settlers from outlaws and unfriendly Indians, at times were used to remove log jams from the Sabine River, and kept a watchful eye over conditions in Texas as it fought for independence from Mexico in 1835 and 1836. When Texas was admitted to the Union in 1845, tensions arose with Mexico over whether the Rio Grande or the Nueces River constituted the border between the two republics. When war broke out in 1846, Fort Jesup served as a supply point for Texas-bound troops. The ranking US officer in the war was by then Gen. Zachary Taylor. Meanwhile, as soon as the military had a strong foothold in Texas, Fort Jesup was abandoned and by the time of the Civil War had fallen to ruin.

In 1957 the state acquired most of the site on which the fort had stood and, after restoring one of the officer's quarters and a kitchen, opened it as **Fort Jesup State Historic Site** (32 Geoghagan Rd., Many; 318-256-4117).

NEW ORLEANS (ORLEANS PARISH)

There would not have been a Wild West, at least not the way it played out, had it not been for the Louisiana Purchase in 1803. That extraordinary land deal put together by President Thomas Jefferson and Secretary of State James Madison gave the young US control of 828,000 square miles (doubling the nation's size) in consideration of $11.25 million paid to France and $3.75 million in assumed debt.

The ceremonies finalizing the transfer of this vast French territory to the US took place in New Orleans—founded in 1718—at the **Cabildo** (701 Chartres St.; 504-568-6968), a three-story structure on Jackson Square next to St. Louis Cathedral. Completed in 1799, the Cabildo (Spanish for "ruling council") still stands. The structure served as a government building during Louisiana's colonial period. Since 1908 it has been the home of the **Louisiana State Museum**, which tells the story of New Orleans, Louisiana, the land deal that would bring Louisiana into the Union, and the rest of the state's colorful, multi-cultural history. In 1988, the historic building was heavily damaged by fire, but following restoration, it reopened in 1994.

Across from the Cabildo is the similar-appearing **Presbytere** (751 Chartres St.; 504-568-6968) begun in 1791 but not completed until 1813. In 1911 it became part of the Louisiana State Museum system.

Less than a decade after the US acquired most of the territory west of the Mississippi, the matter of whether the nation would retain control over all that land was thrown into doubt when Great Britain and the US went to war. The conflict that came to be called the War of 1812 ended shortly after Gen. Andrew Jackson decisively defeated British forces in the January 9, 1815, Battle of Chalmette, better known as the Battle of New Orleans.

The battle site, located five miles from New Orleans, has been preserved as the **Jean Lafitte National Historic Park and Preserve** (8606 West Saint Bernard Hwy., Chalmette; 804-281-0510). A visitor center interprets the battle, while the park's centerpiece is the one-hundred-foot-tall **Chalmette Monument**. The cornerstone for the monument was laid in 1840 to commemorate the twenty-fifth anniversary of the battle, but the obelisk was not completed until 1908.

Had the US not prevailed over Great Britain, historians believe the Mississippi would have become the western border of the nation, leaving what became the Wild West under European control. At least for a time.

Already a major Gulf of Mexico port, following the development of the flat-bottomed steamboats that could navigate the Mississippi and its tributaries, New Orleans became an even more important transportation center. Fittingly enough, the first steamboat to make it down the river to the Crescent City was the *New Orleans*, which was built in Pittsburg in 1811. Soon, hundreds of steamboats were carrying passengers and freight up and down the river and the large waterways that flowed into it. Thanks to this river and Gulf traffic, by 1840, New Orleans was the third largest city in the US. Only New York and Baltimore had more residents.

Though barges and other work vessels still ply the waters of the Mississippi, the steamboat era finally ran aground as railroads began spanning the West. Two replicas of the old-style, four-decked paddle wheelers still operate out of New Orleans, the *Natchez* and the *City of New Orleans*. The **New Orleans Steamboat Company** (400 Toulouse St.; 504-569-1401) offers river cruises on these vessels.

A Friendly Game of Poque

A card game that became a staple of the Wild West—poker—got its figurative first shuffle in New Orleans. Though the game has ancient Chinese roots with modifications by the Persians and later the French, the version that became wildly popular during the American westward movement (and is essentially the same game today) developed in New Orleans.

Long before Louisiana became a state, French settlers in Louisiana were playing a betting game called Poque. As New Orleans began to Americanize, Poque got Anglicized as "poker" and the game grew in popularity faster than a card shark's chip stacks.

New Orleans had its first gambling casino by 1822 (some sources say it was 1827), a club operated by one John Davis that stayed open around the clock. In fact, Davis's establishment became the prototype for the ubiquitous Wild West gambling den—in addition to poker tables he ran roulette wheels, Faro tables, and provided alcoholic beverages and painted ladies.

Gambling had been illegal in Louisiana since 1806, but New Orleans had been exempted from the law. When gambling became illegal in Missouri in 1814, the Crescent City became an even more attractive destination for the sporting trade. The same year, the New Orleans city government began licensing and taxing gaming houses. Twenty years later, the city finally made casinos and other gambling venues illegal. But for decades to come, "illegal" was a relative term in New Orleans.

Thanks to New Orleans riverboat traffic, poker spread via the young nation's extensive river system. The game continued its western expansion by wagon on the Santa Fe, Oregon, and other trails and later with the completion of the first transcontinental railroad. Not only did poker originate in New Orleans, so did a vocation that became as much a part of the Wild West as outlaws and cowboys—the professional gambler. As early as 1834, one Jonathan H. Greer referred to poker as the "cheating game."

Viewing themselves more as entrepreneurs than criminals, card sharks cashed in on the nation's gambling fad. Long before twentieth-century lawmen began using the word "profile" as a synonym for criminal traits, professional gamblers began to fit a certain profile: In addition to knowing all the ways to cheat, they tended to dress nicely, have outgoing personalities (the better to build trust), and preferred resorting to intellectual arguments rather than fisticuffs. Still, aware that some cheated men would not take no for an answer when demanding their money back, they usually toted a concealed weapon, even if it was only a small derringer.

Soon, from boomtown to boomtown across the West, their profession—nonviolent as it usually was—came to be associated with out-of-control crime. Not a few card sharks would get their figurative chips cashed in by dissatisfied players or vigilante committees.

New Orleans' influence on westward expansion involved much more than the popularization of poker. The fast-growing city, which local businessmen believed was well on its way to becoming another New York City, exported cotton, sugar, enslaved people—and revolution.

Businessmen in the Crescent City helped bankroll the 1835–1836 Texas Revolution. The city also sent 120 men, known as the New Orleans Greys, to fight in the revolution. Twenty-three of them died at the Alamo, twenty-one more following the Battle of Goliad. The Texas Navy, whose vessels were obtained and fitted out in New Orleans, helped win the fight. Sam Houston, soon to become president of the new Republic of Texas, came to New Orleans to get medical treatment for the wound he sustained at the Battle of San Jacinto.

The center of the New Orleans effort to support the Texas rebellion against Mexico was **Banks' Arcade**, a three-story, brick commercial center built by wealthy businessman Thomas Banks. The structure, reflective of New Orleans' importance as a commercial center, extended for a full block along Magazine Street, from Gravier to Natchez Streets. A glass-roofed pedestrian passageway extended the full length of the building, an architectural marvel of its day. Capable of accommodating five thousand people, the building included offices, a hotel, shops, a restaurant, bar, and coffee house.

A portion of the arcade still stands, though most of it was destroyed by fire in 1851. Cast-iron galleries were added after to the remaining structure and today it is the **St. James Hotel** (330 Magazine St.; 504-304-4000). The alley behind the hotel, which extends from Gravier to Natchez Streets, tracks the original arcade and is known today as **Arcade Place**. A historic marker outside the entrance to the hotel explains the significance of the site.

Hard to imagine a city of crawfish bisque and powdered sugar–covered beignets as a cattle town, but for a time, it was. For twenty years, cattlemen herded their beeves from *vacheries* (ranches) in southwestern Louisiana to a slaughterhouse in what is now the Garden District. In addition to meat-processing, hides harvested at the plant were shipped to tanneries and tallow went into the making of soap. As New Orleans grew and the focus of the cattle processing industry moved farther west to places like Kansas City and Fort Worth, the Crescent City's two decades as a cattle town came to a close.

With a gumbo-like mixture of history and culture, New Orleans has numerous museums. The **1850 House** (523 St. Ann St.; 504-524-9118), another museum operated by the state, focuses on what daily life was like in the Crescent City in the mid-nineteenth century. Furnished with period art and décor, the museum is part of the Lower Pontalba Building, built by Baroness Micaela Almonester de Pontalba. Her father, Spanish colonial landowner Don Andres Almonester y Roxas, helped finance the Cabildo, the Presbytere, and St. Louis Cathedral.

After coming close to losing New Orleans to the British during the War of 1812, the US began fortifying the narrow straits leading from the Gulf of Mexico to the ever-growing port. One of those installations was Fort Pike, named for Western explorer Zebulon

Pike who had risen in rank to general before being killed in a battle in Canada.

Completed in 1827 after eight years of construction, **Fort Pike** (27100 Chef Menteur Hwy.; 504-662-5703) had two major influences on the Wild West. One, it served in the late 1830s as a stopping point along the so-called Trail of Tears, the route American Indians from the Southeast followed when forced from their homes and relocated to a newly created Indian Territory (future Oklahoma). Secondly, the fort played a role as a military supply facility during the 1846–1848 Mexican War. In winning that war, the US gained control over California and the Southwest. Abandoned in 1890, the old stone fort is now a state historic site and listed on the National Register of Historic Places.

Jackson Barracks, another New Orleans area military post, was built in 1837. Still used by the Louisiana National Guard, the large brick quadrangle, with round towers in each corner, was an important staging area at the beginning of the Mexican War. The **Ansel M. Stroud Jr. Military History and Weapons Museum** (Area C, 4209 Chenault Blvd.; 504-278-8024) is located in the old powder magazine.

While the opening of the West and the Civil War are different epochs, the war between the states clearly had an impact on the subsequent history of the West. New Orleans is home to **Confederate Memorial Hall Museum** (929 Camp St.; 504-523-4522). Opened in 1891, it is Louisiana's oldest museum. Exhibiting flags, uniforms, weapons, and personal items, the museum has the largest collection of Confederate memorabilia in the US. Special exhibits deal with other aspects of Southern military history.

Beginning in December 1884 and continuing until June 1885, New Orleans hosted the **World's Industrial Cotton Centennial Exposition**—essentially a world's fair. Never one to miss a business opportunity, Buffalo Bill Cody staged an extended run of his Wild West show at New Orleans' Oakland Park, since 1914 the site of the **New Orleans County Club** (5024 Pontchartrain Blvd.). While nothing remains of the exhibition site, Buffalo Bill's show had an unusual impact on local culture that continues to this day: When the Wild West show troupe paraded from the exposition grounds through the heart of the city, the procession included several score traditionally attired Plains Indians. With painted faces, war bonnets, and other trappings particular to their tribes, Buffalo Bill's "Congress of Indians" as they were called thrilled the crowd. Many of the city's African-American residents watched the parade and it occurred to someone that dressing up like an American Indian would add a colorful new dimension to the city's annual Mardi Gras celebration. Students of the festival's history say the presence of Buffalo Bill's show in the Crescent City is what inspired what is now known as the Mardi Gras Indians, or Black Masking Indians. The city now has some sixty tribes, African-American social groups who, during Mardi Gras parades, wear lavish costumes derived from American Indian culture.

OPELOUSAS (ST. LANDRY PARISH)

Founded in 1720, Opelousas claims to be the third-oldest city in Louisiana, but history-minded residents of nearby Washington say their town deserves the honor. Regardless of which community merits number-three status, there's plenty of history for all in St. Landry Parish.

Intended as a waypoint on the road from New Orleans to Natchitoches, Opelousas got its start as the site of a Spanish garrison during the time of Spain's control of Louisiana and much of the rest of the land west of the Mississippi. The town was incorporated in 1821 and evolved as an agricultural center. Briefly during the Civil War, it was the state capital.

A Louisiana-raised man who would become one of the Old West's most legendary figures lived with his family in the Opelousas area for roughly five years before going out on his own and eventually leaving the state for Texas.

This man's connection to Opelousas began when Reason and Elve Bowie and their four sons moved there from Catahoula Parish in 1809. The Bowie family raised crops and livestock, much of the labor handled by enslaved workers. Early in 1815, near the end of what became known as the War of 1812, the two oldest Bowie boys, Rezin and James, enlisted to fight the British. But the Battle of New Orleans was fought and won by Gen. Andrew Jackson before the pair could join the fight. Disappointed at missing out on the action, James went on to try a variety of ways to make a living, most of them illegal. His reputation as a fierce fighter was earned in an 1827 incident known as the Sand Bar Fight (see Vidalia, Louisiana). Having already made a couple of trips to Texas, James left Louisiana for good in 1831. Five years later, his name already linked to a fearsome type of knife that saw use across the West, he died when Mexican forces overran the Alamo on March 6, 1836.

The **Opelousas Tourist Information Center** (828 East Landry St.; 337-948-6263) has information on local historical sites (twenty blocks around the parish courthouse have been designated a National Historic District) plus a collection of Jim Bowie–related ephemera. The **Opelousas Museum and Interpretive Center** (315 North Main St.; 337-948-9528) was opened in 1992 and has exhibits telling the city's story. The **Jim Bowie Oak** (133 West Landry St.), adjacent to the 1858 Homere Mouton law office, is more than 350 years old and is registered with the Louisiana Live Oak Society. Behind the oak, the **Jim Bowie Courtyard** is built on the site of what is believed to be a blacksmith shop belonging to the elder Bowie.

Le Vieux Village is a complex of restored historical structures that includes a vintage general store, a doctor's office, two old houses, an early African-American church, a rural schoolhouse, and a railroad depot, all located at the Opelousas Tourist Information Center. The depot houses a museum that tells the story of the so-called **Orphan Trains**, which brought parentless children from New York and other eastern cities for adoption in the West during the nineteenth century. Many of those children came to Opelousas.

RUSTON (LINCOLN PARISH)

Ruston developed in 1883 when the Vicksburg, Shreveport and Pacific Railroad cut across northern Louisiana. As the town grew, so did its crime rate. Realizing that the ready availability of alcohol contributed to the problem, in 1894 the town council passed an ordinance banning sale or possession of alcohol. But that only led to another variety of crime—bootlegging.

One of the more prominent practitioners was Frank Mullins, a professional photographer who found he could make more money developing a whiskey-selling business than he could developing photographs. Before long, deputy US Marshal Tom Sisemore, who also worked as a local law enforcement officer, busted Mullins. That marked the beginning of an antagonistic relationship that would have dire consequences for both men.

On February 28, 1898, Sisemore—by then the town's police chief as well as a federal agent—mortally wounded Mullins in what may or may not have been a justifiable homicide. A jury thought the latter and acquitted the popular chief. But the late Mr. Mullins had friends.

That fall, on November 17, Sisemore came home for supper and after eating spent some time playing with his youngest son. Leaving to make his final rounds through town, he promised to drop off at the post office letters his children had written to Santa Claus. Nearing downtown, he heard a suspicious noise in a nearby pine thicket. Drawing his revolver the lawman walked over to investigate. Suddenly a shotgun went off and the chief fell to the ground as a second blast missed him. Taken to his house, before he died he said he never saw the person who shot him. Despite sizable rewards, the killer was never apprehended. Sisemore family legend had it that someone who had been paid $50 to kill the chief was later hanged for another murder in Arkansas, but that has never been proven.

Chief Sisemore's grave in **Greenwood Cemetery** (intersection of West Alabama Avenue and Everett Street) is marked by a tree-shaped, seven-foot Woodsman of the World monument.

The **Lincoln Parish Museum** (609 North Vienna St.; 318-251-0018) is housed in 1886-vintage Kidd-Davis house and offers exhibits on early Ruston history.

Shreveport (Caddo Parish)

Despite its location at the juncture of the heavily traveled Texas Road—which extended from Missouri to Texas—and the 1,360-mile-long Red River, the site of future Shreveport might have amounted to nothing more than a remote trading post had it not been for a man whose inventions played an important role in the opening of the American West.

Beginning in 1833, as US superintendent of western river improvements, Capt. Henry Miller Shreve used a workhorse riverboat he invented—the *Heliopolis*—along with another steam-powered work boat to clear a nearly two-hundred-mile-long logjam in the Red River. When the federally funded project was completed, for the first time a riverboat could travel from New Orleans up the Red River as far as Texas. The future seat of Caddo Parish, then under development, was named in honor of Shreve, and Shreveport soon prospered as a river port.

Places like Independence and St. Joseph, Missouri, flourished for a time as mid-continent gateways to the West, but 550 miles to the south, thanks to the ingenuity and work ethic of Captain Shreve, the new town became another portal of westward expansion.

The captain did not stay in the town named for him. Instead he settled in St. Louis, where he died in 1851. For whatever reason, he was never photographed, though a portrait painted of him not long after his death was said by his friends to be a good likeness. But not knowing exactly what he looked like did not stop the commissioning in 1967 of artist Arthur Morgan to sculpt a larger-than-life bronze statue of the innovative riverman. The **Henry Miller Shreve statue** stands in front of the appropriately named RiverView Theater and RiverView Hall (600 Clyde Fant Pkwy.).

The **Spring Street Historical Museum** (525 Spring St.; 318-424-0964) covers the history of Shreveport while the **J. Bennett Johnston Waterway Regional Visitors Center** (700 Clyde Fant Pkwy.; 318-

677-2673) focuses on the past and present of the Red River and how the ingenuity of Captain Shreve made the stream navigable.

VIDALIA (CONCORDIA PARISH)

First known as Concord, this town changed its name to Vidalia in honor of **Jose Vidal**, commander from 1798 to 1803 of a Spanish fortification overlooking the Mississippi and just west of the river from Natchez, Mississippi.

What took place on a sandbar between the Louisiana and Mississippi towns on September 9, 1827, was more like the Hollywood version of a Wild West gunfight than many actual Wild West "difficulties."

Dr. Thomas H. Maddox and **Samuel Levi Wells** had agreed to face each other in a pistol duel according to the long-abided by *Code Duello*, or Code of Honor. Each duelist had his supporters and the two factions were as opposed to each other as the duelists. At the appointed time, the duelists faced each other, then turned their backs to walk a few paces before whirling around to again face each other. Each man fired and each man missed. Still following the code, the respective seconds reloaded the handguns for the equivalent of a sudden death playoff. But the combatants missed each other again.

After that, each surely relieved at having satisfied his honor while remaining alive, they shook hands and broke out a bottle of wine. But the supporters of each of the gentlemen were not so willing to let bygones be bygones. They pulled their various weapons—pistols, knifes, and swords—and a general melee ensued.

Two of the antagonists were **James Bowie** and **Norris Wright**. Bowie went down with two bullets in his leg, firing as he fell. Wright drew a sword from his cane and charged Bowie who used his large and soon-to-be famous knife to stab Wright.

"Damn you, Bowie," Wright yelled, "You've killed me!"

Indeed, he had. Another of the combatants also died, but Bowie recovered from his wounds only to die in the Mexican siege of the Alamo in 1836.

The sandbar is long gone, but a historical marker briefly summarizing the incident stands at the intersection of US Highways 65 and 84 in Vidalia. In Marksville, 76 miles from Vidalia, a historical marker on the Avoyelles Parish Courthouse square (312 North Main St.) notes that Bowie's brother, Rezin P. Bowie, wrote, "The first Bowie knife was made by myself in the Parish of Avoyelles."

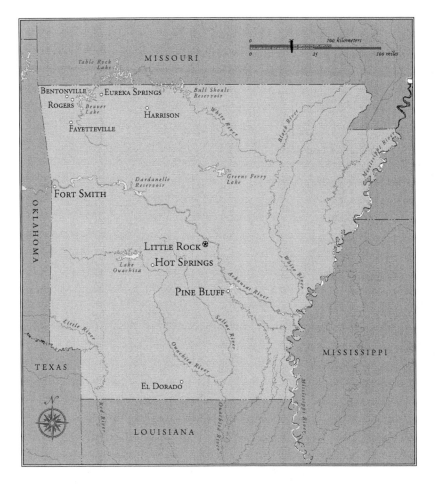

MISSOURI

Table Rock Lake

BENTONVILLE   EUREKA SPRINGS   *Bull Shoals Reservoir*

ROGERS   *Beaver Lake*

HARRISON   *White River*   *Black River*

FAYETTEVILLE

Dardanelle Reservoir   *Greens Ferry Lake*

FORT SMITH

OKLAHOMA

LITTLE ROCK ✪

Lake Ouachita   HOT SPRINGS   *White River*

PINE BLUFF   *Arkansas River*

Little River   *Saline River*   *Mississippi River*

MISSISSIPPI

TEXAS   *Ouachita River*

EL DORADO   MISSISSIPPI

Red River   *Ouachita River*   *Mississippi River*

LOUISIANA

100 kilometers

0   25   100 miles

ARKANSAS

BENTONVILLE (BENTON COUNTY)

Considering what would happen in Bentonville one day in 1893, it doesn't seem all that unusual for the town to have been named for a man known for booze-inspired fistfights and more serious "difficulties" settled with knives or firearms—Thomas Hart Benton. A lawyer by trade, Benton edited a newspaper in St. Louis, Missouri, before turning to politics. When Missouri became a state, Benton went to Washington as its first US senator in 1821 and continued as a powerful political figure for most of the rest of his life. Since he had been a key player in bringing about statehood for Arkansas, when a town was established just seven miles south of the Missouri state line in 1836, it was named for Benton.

Bentonville grew slowly if steadily until the outbreak of the Civil War. In early 1862, Union troops burned down most of the town. The town could have rebounded nicely if the St. Louis and San Francisco Railroad hadn't bypassed it in 1881. Still, there was enough business to support a bank.

The *Benton County Sun* Gets a Big Story

On June 5, 1893, outlaws **Henry Starr** and **Kid Wilson**, along with four cohorts, rode into Bentonville intent on robbing the People's Bank. Unfortunately, at least from the bandits' perspective, several townspeople recognized them.

"Scores of people saw us enter and knew us for bandits. Shooting began the moment we entered the bank," Starr later recalled.

Despite the barrage of bullets, the bandits succeeded in collecting cash and coin. Then, using bank president J. G. McAndrew, cashier George P. Jackson, and two bank directors as human shields, the robbers emerged from the bank with $11,000. They forced Jackson to carry a bag with an additional $900 to $1,000 in silver coins, a burden of about sixty-five pounds.

But as the outlaws and their hostages walked past the nearby office of the *Benton County Sun*, young bookkeeper **Maggie L. Wood** (1864–1953) saw what was happening, opened the door, grabbed Jackson, and pulled him inside. Then she locked the door. The robbers, still under fire from citizens and peace officers, let Jackson and the heavy money bag go. Ditching their remaining hostages, the bandits mounted their horses and galloped out of town with a quickly formed posse not far behind. Despite that, they managed to escape. Twenty-eight years later, trying to rob yet another Arkansas bank, Starr would not be so lucky (see Harrison, Arkansas).

The People's Bank did business in an 1887-vintage building at 101 West Central Avenue, then the most imposing commercial structure in town. Today a restaurant occupies the old bank building. A couple of small dents in one of the metal columns at the entrance are said to be bullet pockmarks dating to the robbery. Outlaw and lawman historian Glen Shirley, who wrote a book on Starr and his exploits, said the 1893 robbery was the biggest thing that ever happened in Bentonville. Despite that, there's no historical marker at the site. However, the **Bentonville History Museum** (306 Northwest 2nd St.; 479-273-3561) has an exhibit on the robbery that includes the original teller cages from the bank. Each year as part of Bentonville's Sugar Creek Days, the robbery shootout is reenacted. Maggie Wood, heroine of the 1893 robbery, is buried in **Bentonville Cemetery** (intersection of Southwest F Street and Southwest 5th Street).

Bentonville isn't only about the bank robbery, though. The **Museum of Native American History** (202 Southwest O St.; 479-273-2456) offers exhibits on the Old West (and even farther back than that). Founded by Bentonville native David Bogle, a registered member of the Cherokee Nation, the museum focuses on the first Americans, from the Paleo period to the Historic period (1650 AD to 1900 AD) with more than ten thousand American Indian artifacts.

BERRYVILLE (CARROLL COUNTY)

The first settler at the site of future Berryville built a cabin there in 1831, but another nineteen years went by before Blackburn H. Berry, late of Alabama, founded the community named for him. (Berry's nephew, James Henderson Berry, became the state's fourteenth governor in 1883.) Like many towns in Arkansas, much of Berryville was burned during the Civil War but the citizenry rebuilt it.

Born in Texas in 1863 during the war, **C. Burton "Buck" Saunders** moved as a child with his family to Berryville, where he grew up. Saunders acquired a reputation as a keen marksman. When he went deer hunting in the Ozarks with an open-sighted Winchester, he often brought home a buck seemingly with no visible wound, until one noticed the bullet hole in its eye. That earned him his nickname.

Saunders headed west as a young man and made big money in real estate, mining, and oil. He began acquiring historic firearms and other relics, but he lost his first collection in the fire that followed the 1906 San Francisco earthquake. Like any dedicated collector, he started all over again.

Over the years, as he and his wife traveled the nation and world, he acquired vintage pistols or rifles associated with Cole Younger, Jesse and Frank James, Wild Bill Hickok, Cherokee Bill, Belle Starr, Buffalo Bill Cody, and other iconic Wild West figures.

Returning to Berryville in 1919 following the death of his wife, Saunders spent the rest of his days there. After he died in 1952, it was revealed that in his will he provided money for the **Saunders Museum** (113 East Madison; 870-423-2563) in which to display his collection of Old West firearms and artifacts.

The **Carroll County Heritage Center** (403 Public Sq.; 870-423-6312) is in the old three-story, red brick Carroll County courthouse, built in 1880 and used for the next ninety-five years. The museum's exhibits focus on all aspects of northwest Arkansas history, from the area's settlement, the Civil War, and agriculture to law and order. The museum also maintains a substantial genealogy collection.

BRINKLEY (MONROE COUNTY)

Brinkley began as a track layer's camp during the construction of Arkansas's first railroad, the Memphis and Little Rock Railroad. First known as Lick Skillet, the town was platted in 1869 and named for railroad president Robert C. Brinkley. Two other rail lines eventually began serving the community, making it a transportation crossroads. While rail traffic has slowed, the town is just south of busy I-40.

Hidden in a Swamp

One of the least known but historically significant sites in the West stands in water several feet deep in the middle of a swamp in the lower delta country of eastern Arkansas.

Twelve years after the Louisiana Purchase was finalized, President James Madison in 1815 ordered an official survey of the nearly nine hundred thousand square miles acquired by the US from France. On November 10 that year, a survey team began working its way north from the confluence of the Arkansas and Mississippi Rivers to establish a north-south line that would be referred to in all future government land claim surveys as the Fifth Principal Meridian. From the junction of the St. Francis and Mississippi Rivers another survey party left about the same time, their mission to shoot an east-west baseline. Where those two imaginary lines crossed was in a still-remote area of what is now Monroe County, Arkansas.

To mark the spot, which would be the starting point for all subsequent surveys of the vast new land west of the Mississippi, the government men blazed marks on two trees. More than a century later, two surveyors re-surveying the boundary between Lee and Phillips Counties in 1921 found the so-called witness trees at the point where the counties of Lee, Monroe, and Phillips intersect. In 1926, the Daughters of the American Revolution placed a gray granite monument on the site. The stone sits right in the middle of the largest headwater swamp still extant in the lower Mississippi valley. Covering an area six miles long and not quite a mile wide, the swamp is the beginning of Cypress Creek.

The Arkansas legislature made the site a state park in 1961, but it was not developed for nearly another two decades. Meanwhile, in 1972 the monument had been listed on the National Register of Historic Places and in 1993 it was designated as a National Historic Landmark. Today, visitors can take a 950-foot boardwalk above the swamp to view the monument, which stands eerily amid moss-covered green water and cypress stumps.

Louisiana Purchase State Park (State Highway 362; 870-572-2352) is a day-use only park. To find it, take US 49 5.2 miles south of Brinkley, then travel 2 miles east on State Highway 362 to the entrance. Watch out for alligators.

CLARKSVILLE (JOHNSON COUNTY)

Named for the first Arkansas territorial judge, Benjamin Johnson, Johnson County was organized in 1833 and Clarksville became county seat three years later. Developing along Spadra Creek, just north of the Arkansas River, the town was a waypoint on the stagecoach lines connecting Little Rock and Fort Smith.

Hanging the Preacher's Son

No one has ever questioned Sidney O. Wallace's name, date of birth, or that he spent his short life in Johnson County, Arkansas. But beyond that, his story is a mixture of folklore and what facts researchers have been able to glean from newspaper coverage and available records. Folklore holds that after the 1863 murder of his preacher father by a gang of bushwhackers who looted their household, Sidney vowed, even at the age of eleven, that it would be him, not the Lord, who exacted vengeance on everyone involved. As a young man he supposedly trailed one of the killers to Kansas and exacted the Biblical "eye for an eye" style of justice on him. Then, at least supposedly, he killed the others who had a hand in his father's death for a total body count of seven by the time he was twenty-two.

More likely is that while his three documented killings did make a certain logic in Wallace's mind, they did not come as retribution against his father's killers. Indeed, the crime that sent him to the gallows was killing Clarksville constable R. W. Ward. That murder, more an assassination, culminated in a violent chain of events that started when Wallace and his brother George—wearing masks—assaulted and attempted to rob two men in 1871. One of those men later killed George Wallace, and the human "dominoes" continued to fall until Sid Wallace's well-attended public execution in Clarksville on March 13, 1874. Some came to even doubt that he died that day, the legend persisting that his hanging had been faked.

Wallace is buried in Clarksville's **Oakland Memorial Cemetery** (402 Cemetery St.; 479-754-8271). Just as there are two versions of how Wallace ended up at the end of a rope, he has two tombstones as well. The first is an old marker, clearly dating to shortly after his execution. The second is a more contemporary gray granite tombstone. Johnson County has ten state historical markers, but none mention Wallace, his victims, or his hanging.

Also buried in Oakland Memorial Cemetery is **Paden Tolbert** (1862–1904). As a deputy US marshal based in Fort Smith, Arkansas, Tolbert did most of his work in Indian Territory. He earned a reputation for effectiveness and lasting fame in leading the posse that killed Cherokee outlaw **Ned Christie** in 1892. Tolbert died on April 24, 1904, of natural causes in Hot Springs, Arkansas, just shy of his forty-second birthday, but he was buried in Clarksville where his family lived. By the mid-twentieth century, the four-foot gray granite obelisk over his grave needed repair. The monument was reinforced and in something of a rarity when it comes to early Western tombstones, more verbiage was added, including the fact that October 26, 1958, had been designated Paden Tolbert Day in Johnson County.

Another noted figure from Johnson County's past is **William M. "Bill" Doolin**, born to a sharecropper family near Clarksville in 1858. In his early twenties, Doolin left home for Indian Territory in what is now Oklahoma and took up cowboying. But then he fell in with bad company. Meeting outlaw Emmett Dalton while working on a ranch near present Pawnee, Oklahoma, in 1891, he transitioned from wrangling cattle to robbing trains. He rode with the infamous Dalton gang until most of its members were killed trying to rob a bank in Coffeeville, Kansas, in 1892. Then he formed his own outlaw cabal, a group that came to be known as **Doolin's Wild Bunch** (not to be confused with the famed Butch Cassidy's Wild Bunch). In 1892 Doolin survived a bloody shootout with deputy US marshals in Ingalls, Oklahoma Territory, but he would not live to old age (see Eureka, Arkansas).

Operated by the Johnson County Historical Society, the **Johnson County Heritage Center Museum** (131 West Main St.; 479-754-3334) has exhibits and archival records related to the county's history.

DANVILLE (YELL COUNTY)

Most towns are named for a pioneer or nearby geographic feature, but Danville is named after a steamboat that once navigated the Petit Jean River, a 131-mile stream flowing into the Arkansas River. Settled in 1841 following the creation of Yell County the year before, the west-central Arkansas town was incorporated in 1899. It was the setting for Charles Portis's novel *True Grit*, a book later made into the movie that won longtime Western star John Wayne his only Oscar for his portrayal of fictional US Marshal Rooster Cogburn.

All on Account of Pigs

Yell County was the setting for a little-known but particularly ugly feud between the families of brothers Jack and Bud Daniels and **William Potter** and their respective allies. What started in 1882 over an accusation of pig purloining would claim six lives and alter many more.

The violence began April 19, 1883, when **Russell Jackson "Jack" Daniels**, his brother **John W. "Bud" Daniels**, and a friend,

George Riley Blocker, showed up at Potter's place. One version holds that Potter, who suspected the Danielses of having rustled some of his hogs, got himself killed in self-defense by going for his rifle. Potter's widow said the brothers and their ally murdered her husband (it took him two hours to die) in cold blood. If it really had been a matter of kill or be killed, the brothers Daniel and Blocker did not stay around to argue their case. Instead, they headed to the hills in a remote area locally known as "Three Corners" because the boundaries of Yell, Garland, and Montgomery Counties converged there. Soon newspapers began calling the fugitives the "Three Corners Desperadoes."

On July 29, a posse of deputies and volunteers led by area county sheriffs rode into an ambush and came under fire from the fugitives. Potter's brother-in-law, Shelton Conway, was shot and killed while posse member Charles D. Carter suffered a mortal wound and died August 7.

Blocker surrendered to authorities early in August, but the Daniels brothers remained on the lam. Meanwhile, John H. Coker and Dr. John Flood were separately arrested for having harbored the two suspects. Coker also was suspected of setting up the earlier attack on the sheriff's posse.

The three men were awaiting due process when on the night of September 9 more than a dozen masked men forced their way into the lockup, used an ax to break the locks on their cells, and took charge of Coker and Flood. Content to let the judicial system handle Blocker, the vigilantes took Coker and Flood to the nearby iron bridge spanning the Petit Jean River and lynched them from it.

Blocker, likely worried the vigilantes would change their mind and come back for him, broke out of jail soon after the double lynching. Recaptured about a month later, he escaped a second time and was never seen again, at least not in Yell County. Neither were the Daniels brothers.

The sixth and final fatality connected to the feud came December 14, when Mrs. Jack Daniels, her husband in hiding and with no means to support their six children, used a rifle to shoot herself in the heart.

The bridge from which Coker and Flood were hanged continued in use until it was replaced in 1920. The old "bow string"
bridge, a hundred feet long, was stored until 1922, when it was
placed across the river at Mickles, Arkansas. In 2013 it was
moved to a spot near the Danville City Hall and mounted on
concrete pillars.

William O. "Bill" Potter is buried in the **Killian Cemetery**
(Chula Road near Aly in Yell County; GPS coordinates: N34°
47.634', W93° 30.414'). Charles Carter lies in the **Brearley
Cemetery** (Quay Street at Meers Lane, Dardanelle; GPS coordinates: N35° 13.200', W93° 10.266'). Engraved on the base of
his elaborate monument is a flowery sixty-eight-word summary
of the circumstances surrounding his demise. Caldwell is buried
in the **Caldwell Cemetery** (Mount Tabor; GPS coordinates: N34°
44.214', W93° 17.514'). The location of Wood's and Coker's
graves is unknown.

EL DORADO (UNION COUNTY)

Matthew Rainey opened a general store here in 1843 in the piney
woods of Southern Arkansas, and a small settlement soon developed
around it. He named it El Dorado, after the Southwest's legendary
city of gold—a place that had existed only in the collective imagination of early Spanish explorers. The same year Rainey arrived, the
community was designated the county seat. It remained a small town
until the railroad arrived in the 1890s and then El Dorado prospered
for a time as a timber shipping point.

A particularly sanguinary period of violence in El Dorado that
came to be known as the **Tucker-Parnell Feud** began in 1902 and continued into 1905. Though technically unfolding in the early twentieth
century, the gunplay was a throwback to the heyday of the Wild West.

The feud has been the subject of two nonfiction books, but to
distill a long story, it began because two Arkansas men—one from
out of town, one local—wanted to marry the same woman. When
the local man assaulted his nonresident rival, the out-of-towner asked

city marshal **Guy Tucker** for protection. The marshal stood by as the man hastily married the young lady in question, and then escorted the newlyweds to the train station. Meanwhile, constable **Harrison Dearing** arrested the jilted suitor for assault. But when the man was released on bail the following day, he confronted Dearing. The fight that ensued ended with the constable shooting and mortally wounding the local man.

That man happened to be a family friend of local resident **Marshall Parnell**, father of eight sons. The Parnells were angry with the constable for killing their pal, and also highly irritated with Marshal Tucker. Beyond the death of the Parnells' friend, the family thought Tucker had unfairly enforced a city ordinance as it pertained to a sidewalk in front of a store the Parnells owned. Further complicating things was the pending grand jury testimony of one of the Parnells regarding the shooting of their friend. It all came to a head on October 9, when gunfire broke out on the courthouse square. When the smoke cleared, Constable Dearing and two of the Parnell boys lay dead.

The feud continued, including attempted killings and successful killings, through 1905. Before feelings calmed down, an estimated thirty to forty deaths had occurred in Union County.

Two metal historical markers summarize the bloodiest day of the feud, the October 9, 1902, gunfight on the courthouse square. One marker features a map showing the location of the participants in the shootout and the other briefly tells the story of the feud. Both markers are located on the west side of the square at 111 North Jefferson Avenue. Four Parnells killed during the feud, William Thomas (1855–1902), Walter W. (1873–1902), John F. (1871–1903), and Lenox (1885–1903), are buried in **Wyatt-Parnell Cemetery** (Parnell Road, northeast of its intersection with Del-Tin Highway). In the 1980s, the feud long since a matter of history and no longer anything personal for anyone, the shootout began to be reenacted for the benefit of tourists. Evolving into a theatrical presentation known as the *Showdown at Sunset,* the gunplay that left three dead and three wounded is reenacted every Saturday, June through August.

A two-story Greek Revival–style house built around 1849 by early residents John and Penelope Newton is the oldest structure in El Dorado. For years the house was assumed to have been built by town founder Matthew Rainey, but later research showed that while Rainey sold the Newtons the land on which the house stands, he didn't build it or ever live there. Listed on the National Register of Historic Places, in 1978 the house was purchased by the South Arkansas Historical Preservation Society, which restored it and turned it into the **Newton House Museum** (510 North Jackson Ave.; 870-862-9890).

Eureka Springs (Carroll County)

Dr. Alvah Johnson believed the warm, mineral-laden water saved his son's vision. Or at least that's what he claimed when he began selling Dr. Johnson's Eye Water from Basin Spring in 1856. Word of the spring's supposed healing properties steadily spread, and the hilly town of Eureka Springs bubbled to life on July 4, 1879. By the mid-1880s Eureka Springs had developed as a resort town with numerous hotels and bathhouses. The town attracted all types, good and bad.

Eureka, Indeed

Arkansas-born outlaw Bill Doolin had been bothered by rheumatism ever since getting shot in the leg following a train robbery near Cimarron, Kansas. A doctor suggested that soaking in the hot mineral water of Eureka Springs might help his condition and Doolin took him up on it. While the wanted bandit may have been acting on good medical advice, he did not realize that deputy US Marshal Bill Tilghman had figured out that Doolin was headed for Eureka. The marshal arrived in Eureka at mid-morning January 15, 1896. Walking uptown from the train station, Tilghman almost immediately saw Doolin on the street. Luckily, Doolin did not notice him.

The marshal found a carpenter and commissioned him to build something that looked like a packing box so he could conceal his shotgun in it. But as it turned out, he would not need the handheld Trojan horse, clever an idea though it was. Entering one of the bathhouses to take a relaxing dip himself, the federal lawman again ran into Doolin, who was sitting in the lounge reading a newspaper. Pretending not to notice him, Tilghman rushed past the fugitive toward another room. Closing the door behind him, the marshal drew his pistol, watched through a crack in the door until Doolin again had his nose in the newspaper, and then burst in to make the arrest. Soon the marshal and his prisoner were on a train headed back to Oklahoma Territory. What became of the custom shotgun case is not known.

Eureka Springs once had more than two score hotels and bathhouses. While the bathhouse where Tilghman arrested Doolin no longer stands, two of the old bathhouses remain. The only one still in operation is the **Palace Hotel and Bath House** (135 Spring St.), which opened in 1901. While not in operation as a bathhouse, the other survivor of the town's mineral waters heyday is the **Basin Springs Bath House** (Main and Spring Streets). Built in 1889, this four-story brick building was gutted by fire in 1986 but restored and reopened in 1987 as business space.

With numerous stone Victorian buildings, including the **1886 Crescent Hotel**, the entire town is listed on the National Register of Historic Places. For an overview of the city, visit the **Eureka Springs Visitor Center** (137-A West Van Buren; 479-253-9572).

Located in the 1889 Calif House, the **Eureka Springs Historical Museum** (95 South Main St.; 479-253-9417) tells the story of this once robust resort town that for a time was Arkansas's fourth-largest city.

FAYETTEVILLE (WASHINGTON COUNTY)

Fayetteville got off to a rough start. Other than being on the edge of the Western frontier when it was first settled in the late 1820s, the community lay at a crossroad of several long-established Indian trails that Euro-American travelers had begun to use. The most-traveled trail stretched from Jefferson City, Missouri, to Fort Smith, Arkansas. The routes brought settlers and trade, but they also brought trouble.

"Shooting, stabbing, knocking down and dragging out appear to be the order of the day," one resident wrote in 1840. "Everyone you see is armed to the teeth." To mitigate the situation, a vigilante group known as the **Committee of 36** began running undesirables out of town and if that failed, lynching them.

When the Butterfield Overland Mail Company began carrying people and mail from St. Louis to California in 1858, it passed through Fayetteville en route to Fort Smith along the well-used military road that had once been an Indian trail.

After the Civil War, Fayetteville became the home of Arkansas Industrial University (forerunner of the University of Arkansas), which opened in 1872. Once the town had a railroad connection, it grew as a cultural and economic center of northeastern Arkansas.

Fayetteville's original courthouse square was torched during the Civil War, but the city has numerous Victorian-era buildings and residences. A walking tour of downtown historic sites is available from the **Washington County Historical Society** (118 East Dickson St.; 479-512-2970). Located in the 1853-vintage **Jonas and Matilda Tibbetts House,** the society operates a museum there focused on the city and county's history.

Adjacent to the museum is the restored **Archibald Yell law office,** built around 1835. Yell served variously as a judge, a member of Congress, governor, and soldier. The one-story frame cabin was moved from its original location to the museum property in 1992 and is open to visitors along with the **Ridge House** (230 West Center St.). Built in 1839 by a member of the Cherokee Nation named John Ridge, the house became the refuge of Sara Bird Northrup Ridge after her husband was killed in Indian Territory by another Cherokee. The restored house is also owned by the historical society.

FORT SMITH (SEBASTIAN COUNTY)

One of the Wild West's gateway cities, Fort Smith began with the establishment of a US Army post on a bend of the Arkansas River in 1817. However, the community's primary influence on the frontier had to do with the judiciary, not the military. From 1873 to 1896, the US Court for the Western District of Arkansas sat at Fort Smith with jurisdiction over Indian Territory, which then covered much of what later became the state of Oklahoma. That made the court unique in American judicial history. While most federal judges generally hear civil matters, the Fort Smith court handled thousands of criminal cases emanating from the adjacent and, for a time, a very violent Indian Territory.

"Hanging Judge" **Isaac C. Parker** presided over the court from 1875 to 1896. He sentenced 160 people to death during his tenure, though not quite half that number ended their days on the gallows. Newspapers and writers of sensationalized books dubbed him the "Hanging Judge," but the record shows that all Parker sought to do was properly dispense justice. He was a particularly strong supporter of Indian rights and not as punishment-minded as he has been portrayed. Parker died November 17, 1896, at the age of fifty-eight and is buried in **Fort Smith National Cemetery** (522 Garland Ave.; 479-783-5345; section 9, grave 4000). His modest white marble tombstone, bearing only the grave number "4000" and his name, belies the tremendous influence he had in bringing law and order to what is now Oklahoma. He is buried next to his wife.

William Henry Harrison Clayton served as Judge Parker's chief prosecutor. Clayton and his family lived in an 1850s-vintage three-story frame house from 1882 to 1897. Before occupying it, Clayton enlarged and remodeled it in the Victorian Gothic Italianate style of the day. With more than 6,000 square feet of floor space, the house had eight main rooms, each warmed with a coal-burning heater. While the Victorian furniture on display was not used by the Claytons, the house does feature several artifacts dating to the family's occupancy. **The Clayton House** (514 North 6th St.) is located in the twenty-three-block **Belle Grove Historic District** and is open to the public and maintained by the Fort Smith Heritage Foundation, which saved it from demolition in 1969.

The bodies of the seventy-nine prisoners hanged on Judge Parker's order were returned to their families if possible. But the remains of twenty-eight condemned men went unclaimed and were buried in the potter's field section of **Oak Cemetery** (1401 South Greenwood Ave.). Only one of those men, Shepard Busby, has a tombstone. Hanged on April 27, 1892, his grave is number 668 in block 11/13.

In 1846, when Indians no longer posed a threat to Arkansas, the War Department converted Fort Smith into a military supply depot. The facility had two officer's quarters, a barracks, a commissary, and a storehouse. After the army permanently abandoned the post in 1872, the brick commissary became a federal courthouse. The former barracks served as offices for the court clerk, US marshal, and the US commissioner. Prisoners were held in a jail in the basement of the courthouse/commissary. Nearby, the government constructed the gallows that would see plenty of use over the next twenty-three years. Two federal judges who presided in Fort Smith prior to Judge Parker's appointment ordered the hanging of seven men from 1873 to when Parker took over in 1875, for a total of eighty-six men hanged in thirty-nine executions through 1896. On two different occasions, six men were hanged simultaneously. When the Western District of Arkansas's jurisdiction in Indian Territory ended in 1896, the gallows were torn down and most of the timbers burned.

With black-and-white Westerns dominating prime time television in the mid-1950s, Fort Smith civic leaders realized the town could cash in on the Wild West craze by restoring Judge Parker's courtroom and, better yet, the gallows from which several score of men were hanged during his time on the bench. A replica of the gallows was ready by the time school ended for the summer in 1957.

The National Park Service took over the property in 1961 and opened the restored courthouse and other features to the public in 1963 as the **Fort Smith National Historic Site** (301 Parker Ave.; 479-783-3961). The original 1957 replica of the gallows, patterned after newspaper descriptions and an 1886 photograph, stood for twenty-four years until the National Park Service built a new replica in 1981 where it had originally stood. (A warehouse that had been built on the site had been razed as part of the park service's efforts to recreate the old federal complex.) For years, nooses with the iconic hangman's knot dangled from the gallows, but in 2014 the Park Service decided it would be more tasteful to display the ropes only on the anniversary dates of notable executions.

The Hangman's Daughter

George Maledon (1830–1911) could not have been pleased to learn that his twenty-four-year-old daughter Annie had fallen for Frank Carver, a man then on trial before Judge Parker for smuggling whiskey into Indian Territory. A former Fort Smith peace officer and federal employee who had overseen the hanging of dozens, Maledon knew a bad man when he saw one. But when Carver's trial ended, Annie joined him when he returned to Muskogee in Indian Territory. There, she soon discovered Carver had forgotten to tell her he had an Indian wife. Confronting her drunken paramour on March 25, 1895, Annie was shot for her trouble. Gravely wounded, she was taken back to Fort Smith where she died on May 19.

Carver was tried for murder, convicted, and sentenced to death. But his lawyer succeeded in getting that conviction overturned. While another jury convicted him again, it was for the lesser offense of manslaughter.

Though his daughter's murder is little-known, the German-born Maledon came to be called the Prince of Hangmen. Maledon did hang the majority of those sentenced to death by Judge Parker while employed by the US Marshal's Service (he did not work directly for Judge Parker), but writers have considerably exaggerated his story. Devastated by the loss of his daughter and the outcome of Carver's case, Maledon soon left Fort Smith hoping to capitalize on his gruesome reputation with a macabre traveling show by displaying nooses, pieces of the recently dismantled gallows, and photographs taken at some of his hangings. He ended his days at an old soldier's home in Tennessee.

Annie Maledon is buried with five other family members in **Calvary Cemetery** (715 Lexington Ave.). Records show her unmarked grave lies to the immediate left of her mother Elizabeth Maledon's grave, which does have a stone.

The Night of the Lingerie Parade

The three-story clapboard building with wrought-iron-trimmed mansard roof and dormer windows standing in downtown Fort Smith has been accommodating the public in one way or the other since its construction in 1896. First operated as the **Riverfront Commercial Hotel**, the structure was purchased by Miss Laura Ziegler in 1898 with $3,000 in borrowed money. She renovated the building and opened it as a brothel in 1903, repaying her loan after only seventeen months in business.

Miss Laura's house enjoyed the reputation of being the highest-class establishment on "The Row," as the rough river town's red-light district was known. Business began to slow at the beginning of the twentieth century's second decade, a decline accelerated on January 7, 1910, when an oil storage tank blew up, burning down two brothels and damaging others. The fire came during peak evening business hours, the event becoming known as "the night of the lingerie parade." Wisely, a year later Zigler sold out to a woman known as "Big Bertha," a madame not as picky with her staff or clientele. The house continued as a seedy place of prostitution until 1948 and slid even more downhill after that. By 1963 it stood abandoned and in danger of being torn down by order of the city. A history-minded buyer saved the building from demolition, and in 1973 it went on the National Register of Historic Places, making it the only former bordello in the state to be listed. Restored in 1983, it operated as a restaurant until 1992, when it became the **Fort Smith Visitor Center** (2 North B St.). A tornado took off the original roof in the spring of 1996, but the old baroque Victorian building was restored to its original appearance, complete with period wallpaper and furnishings.

Bass Reeves Monument

Dedicated in 2012, a twenty-five-foot bronze monument in downtown Fort Smith honors **Bass Reeves**, the Wild West's best known African-American lawman. The larger-than-life work of public art, *Into the Territory* (Ross Pendercraft Park, 200 Garrison St.), commemorates the life of a larger-than-life man. Sculpted by Harold T. Holden, the statue depicts Reeves, rifle in hand, gazing west across the Arkansas River toward Indian Territory with his faithful tracking dog at the ready alongside his horse. Born into slavery in 1838, Reeves grew up in Grayson County, Texas, just south of the Red River from Indian Territory.

The first black deputy US marshal to serve west of the Mississippi, Reeves was appointed in 1875 and held the dangerous job for thirty-two years. Illiterate, but fluent in several American Indian languages, he memorized arrest warrants and usually returned with the criminals he sought. He arrested more than three thousand men and women, including his own son—charged with murder for killing Reeves's daughter-in-law. The son, and most of the other defendants Reeves took into custody, did not resist. Known by many as "the Reverend," Reeves referred fourteen wanted men who violently demurred to a higher court. Of those line-of-duty killings, one led to a murder charge against Reeves, but he was acquitted before Judge Parker. After Oklahoma became a state in 1907, Reeves joined the Muskogee Police Department and worked as an officer for two years. After retiring due to failing health, he died in 1910.

US Marshals Museum

After a nationwide selection process, Fort Smith was chosen in 2007 as the location of a planned museum dedicated to the long and colorful history of the US Marshal Service, established with congressional passage of the Judiciary Act in 1789. Overlooking the Arkansas River, the fifty-three-thousand-square-foot, star-shaped **US Marshals Museum** (789 Riverfront Dr.; 479-709-3766) opened in the fall of 2019. In addition to documenting the action-filled history of the service, the museum honors the more than two hundred federal marshals and deputy marshals killed in the line of duty since the agency's founding. More than half of the lawmen killed—109—died in what is now Oklahoma. Most of those deaths occurred during Judge Parker's stint on the bench.

HAMBURG (ASHLEY COUNTY)

Founded in 1849 as the county seat of newly created Ashley County, Hamburg is the burial place of **Charles Portis** (1933–2020), author of the classic Western novel *True Grit*.

Born fifty-nine miles west of Hamburg in El Dorado, after service in the US Marine Corps during the Korean War, Portis studied journalism at the University of Arkansas in Fayetteville. As a young newspaperman in Little Rock, he was struck by the strong personalities of some of the small-town, elderly female country correspondents he dealt with and later said he incorporated some of their personality traits into his character Mattie Ross.

Set in western Arkansas and the Indian Territory, *True Grit* is the story of young Mattie's efforts to find the man who killed her father—assisted by a hard-drinking, hard-fighting deputy US Marshal Rooster Cogburn and a Texas Ranger. The book was published in 1968 and the following year was adapted for the screen with John Wayne as the marshal and singer Glen Campbell as the ranger. The movie, for which Wayne won his only Oscar, is considered by film critics and fans to be among the best-ever Westerns. In its listing of the top one hundred best Westerns, the movie review website Rotten Tomatoes has the 1969 film as the twenty-first most popular with the 2010 remake starring Jeff Bridges as the seventh most popular.

Portis died in 2020 at the age of eighty-six and is buried in **Hamburg Cemetery** (East Parker Street and Eugene Hill Road).

Located in a two-story brick house more than a century old, the **Ashley County Museum** (302 North Cherry St.; 870-853-2244) focuses on the history and culture of the county and Hamburg.

HARRISON (BOONE COUNTY)

Only four years after the Civil War, the people of newly organized Boone County named their county seat for a Yankee officer. The area had been devastated during the war and during Reconstruction, when yet-unreconstructed Southerners did not cotton to pro-Union folks. Accordingly, the Unionists succeeded in getting the new county of Boone created from the eastern half of Rebel-leaning Carroll County. Col. Marcus LaRue Harrison, who was in the vicinity surveying a railroad route, agreed to lay out a townsite that would be named in his honor. The town was incorporated in 1876.

In April 1857 a wagon train of 120-plus men, women, and children left future Boone County for a new start in distant California. They never made it. The party included about forty families from Carroll, Crawford, Johnson, and Marion Counties in northwest Arkansas.

Formed in the vicinity of Beller's Stand, just south of present Harrison, the wagon train is most commonly referred to as the **Baker-Fancher Train**. Capt. Alexander Fancher, who had made two previous trips to California, led the slow-rolling entourage. Likely joined by a few other families along the way, the party made it as far as Utah Territory. There they split into two groups. The emigrants who opted to take the southern route to California were attacked on September 7 by a combined force of Paiutes and the Mormon militiamen who had recruited them. (That US citizens would be attacking their fellow countrymen was connected to the so-called Mormon War, in which the US military sent troops into Utah Territory, and resentment over the death of a Mormon leader in Arkansas a few months before.) Following a standoff that lasted four days, the travelers were finally overwhelmed and slaughtered. A monument to the victims of what came to be called the **Mountain Meadows Massacre** was placed in 1955 on the lawn of the Boone County Courthouse (169 North Main St.).

To learn more about the area, start at the **Arkansas Welcome Center** (3391 US 65; 870-741-3343).

Caught a Shooting Starr

When **Henry Starr** became a bank robber, and turned to a life of crime, he was just taking up the family business. His grandfather, Tom Starr, and his aunt by marriage, Belle Starr, also were well-known Oklahoma outlaws during the 1870s and 1880s. Henry Starr robbed his first bank in 1891, and though he periodically claimed reformation, he pulled at least twenty-one bank jobs during a career lasting nearly three decades.

His run ended in this Ozark Mountain town in north central Arkansas. Here, on February 18, 1921, Starr and two associates walked into People's National Bank and ordered everyone into the vault. Former bank president William J. Myers happened to be there that day. Unfortunately for Starr, years earlier Myers had "deposited" a Winchester rifle in the vault just for such a contingency as now arose. Myers entered the vault as ordered but grabbed the rifle and shot Starr. When the robber went down, his two accomplices ran outside and sped off in their car. In addition to being Starr's last robbery, the crime is believed to have been the first in which an automobile was used for the getaway.

Built circa 1900, the brick building that was the home of People's National Bank when Starr tried to rob it—though altered by remodeling—still stands at the southeast corner of Stephenson and Willow on the courthouse square in Harrison. A metal plaque on the building's front tells the story of the incident that closed Starr's career.

Starr died in the **Boone County Jail** (Central Avenue and Willow Street) four days after the failed holdup. The two-story, red brick lockup was built in 1914 and still stands. It was listed on the National Register of Historic Places in 1976.

The **Boone County Heritage Museum** (124 South Cherry St.; 870-741-3312) has extensive holdings related to Henry Starr, including a .38-caliber bullet extracted from the outlaw and the Model 1873 lever-action Winchester rifle from which that piece of lead came. The slug flattened when it hit the bank robber's spine. In addition to numerous photographs of Starr and the former banker who shot him, the museum's collection includes the death bed confession prosecutor Karl Greenhaw took from Starr on February 21, 1921. Starr and three witnesses signed it. The museum is in the old Harrison High School, a three-story brick building that dates to 1912.

The shootout with Starr was not the town's first noted gunfight. On December 24, 1897, downtown was crowded with Christmas shoppers when a gunfight broke out on the southeast corner of the courthouse square. When the shooting stopped, **Monroe L. Alderhalt** lay mortally wounded, hit by two rounds from a revolver. Even so, he had managed to get off four shots at his assailants before he fell. Three younger men, brothers **Frank, Henry,** and **Troy Pace,** were arrested shortly after the shooting, which many had witnessed. Alderhalt died early Christmas morning. Frank and Henry were soon charged with first-degree murder and Troy was charged with assault. The Pace family was well thought of in the community. Alderhalt, however, was described by one newspaper as a "fearless and desperate man." The defendants in the case never went to trial. The deadly holiday difficulty, a local historian later wrote, was one of at least twenty gunfights on or near the southeast corner of the courthouse square. The intersection came to be called Deadman's Corner.

HOT SPRINGS (GARLAND COUNTY)

Attracted by thermal springs spouting mineral-rich water at a constant 143 degrees, people have been coming to this area since pre-historic times. By the early 1830s, the town that grew around the springs had become a resort city—the nation's first. Not surprisingly, it came to be called Hot Springs. But despite its reputation as a place of relaxation and physical rejuvenation, Hot Springs could be a decidedly unhealthy place, especially for gamblers, gents who took exception to a stacked deck, rival casino operators, and lawmen, both honest and crooked.

Jesse and **Frank James**, two of the Wild West's most noted outlaws, may have robbed their first stagecoach about five miles from Hot Springs on January 15, 1874. Also believed to have been in on the heist were Cole and Bob Younger. Taken in the holdup were cash and personal valuables. While it was never definitely determined that the James-Younger gang pulled this robbery, one source says a gold watch taken that day was found among Jesse James's effects after his death.

A decade later, another noted Wild West episode had to do with a different way to relieve people of their money—gambling. Hot Springs gambling boss **Frank Flynn** controlled the city's gaming establishments. When former partner **Jim Lane** opened two competing gambling halls, Flynn and his henchmen violently forced Lane out of town. But Lane was determined to get his cut of the resort's lucrative gambling trade. To that end, he retained the services of Major S. A. (Alex) Doran, a Confederate veteran turned itinerate professional gambler whose post-war enemies were anyone who annoyed him or whose death would be financially remunerative. In consideration of $6,000, Lane hired Doran to get rid of Flynn one way or another. The territorial war, which a bloodless duel between Flynn and Doran failed to resolve (Flynn missed Doran and while Doran did shoot Flynn, a protective metal vest stopped the bullets), culminated in a wild downtown shootout on February 9, 1884. The battle left three men dead and three wounded. During the protracted street fight between the Doran and Flynn gangs, more than a hundred rounds were fired. The leaders of both factions survived the engagement, but it marked the beginning of the end of Flynn's ruthless gambling monopoly. It also set the stage for an even bloodier gun battle fifteen years later. A bronze plaque imbedded in the sidewalk along Central Avenue (GPS coordinates: N34° 30.74', W93° 03.26') across from the Buckstaff Bathhouse marks the site of the Flynn-Doran shootout.

Wide-open gambling and prostitution are civic blights by most people's standards, but when local police officers get into a gunfight with sheriff's deputies the situation has clearly gotten out of hand. That's what happened in the heart of Hot Springs on March 16, 1899. Police Chief **Thomas C. Toler** (a lawman who had succeeded in stopping the Flynn-Doran fight before even more people died) and some of his officers shot it out with Garland County Sheriff **Bob Williams** and some of his deputies. When the smoke cleared, Toler and three of his officers lay dead or dying and one deputy had been killed. In addition to the five fatalities, one deputy had been wounded along with a civilian bystander who caught a stray bullet. Though the fight had not been planned and spun out of control over heated words, the bloodshed was essentially a confrontation between the pro-gambling faction (Police Chief Toler and his men) and those with a desire to honestly uphold the rule of law (Sheriff Williams and his deputies). Several, including the sheriff, stood trial in connection with that day's events but no convictions resulted. The battle severely impacted the city's tourist industry for a time, and ill feelings between city and county law enforcement lasted well into the twentieth century.

Start your visit to the area at the **Hot Springs Visitor Center** (629 Central Ave.; 800-772-2489).

Legend has it that a cave, now part of **DeSoto Park** (1700 Park Ave.), was a Jesse James gang hideout. He and his colleagues supposedly also rested up from their crimes by soaking in the hot springs that gave the town its name.

Hot Springs National Park (369 Central Ave.; 501-620-6715) was established to preserve natural features, but it also pays homage to the history of the West. It is, as the National Park Service puts it,

"Where history and nature meet." President Thomas Jefferson dispatched two scientists to report on the springs in 1804. Twenty-eight years later, in 1832, long before the creation of the national park system, the US government set aside the area around the springs as a federal reserve.

Founded in 1960, the **Garland County Historical Society** (328 Quapaw Ave.; 501-321-2159) curates more than sixty-six thousand photographs, documents, and maps related to the history of Hot Springs and Garland County. The archive also has extensive holdings on the town's violent past. In addition, the center features interpretive exhibits and artifacts ranging from early-day gambling paraphernalia to antique surveying equipment.

The Wild West era survived in Hot Springs well into the twentieth century. While the **Gangster Museum of America** (510 Central Ave.; 501-318-1717) focuses on the mobsters who frequented the resort in the 1920s, '30s, and '40s, the illegal gambling that drew them to the Ozarks got its start in the previous century.

LITTLE ROCK (PULASKI COUNTY)

Making his way along the Arkansas River in 1722, a Frenchman named Bernard de la Harpe noted on the west bank a small rock formation that stood out. He named it La Petite Roche. Since a Quapaw Indian village stood near it, La Harpe decided to establish a trading post there. In time, La Harpe left but the place name he had come up with endured, albeit in English.

In 1812, a trapper named William Lewis built a cabin near Little Rock. By 1819, when Arkansas became a territory, a small community had developed around Lewis's cabin. A year later, a townsite was platted as Little Rock and in 1821 the capital was moved there. The first steamboat called at Little Rock in 1822 and with its status as capital, the still small town was on its way to becoming the state's commercial center.

American politics has always been contentious, and that was certainly true during Arkansas's territorial days. Proving that politicians are capable of arguing about anything, in December 1837 House Speaker John Wilson—on the floor of the House chamber—had a difference of opinion with Representative J.J. Anthony over a proposed bill providing for a bounty on the wolves that could still be found throughout the territory. Wilson settled the matter with a Bowie knife, ending Anthony's political career and his life. Wilson was expelled from the General Assembly, tried for murder, and acquitted. He was later voted back into office.

Little Rock endured the vagaries of the Civil War and political violence during Reconstruction but continued to grow at a slow but mostly steady pace. After getting its first rail connection in 1872, the city became a transportation center and business hub.

Like all riverboat towns, Little Rock had a waterfront strip of bars and bordellos known locally as Battle Row. Kate Merrick's place, the **Ocean Wave**, was the most popular of the pleasure palaces. The Ocean Wave crested when fire destroyed it in April 1879. The loss of the Ocean Wave and the demise of riverboat traffic ended the red-light district, though it would be years before open prostitution disappeared completely.

Little Rock Visitors Center (615 East Capitol Ave.; 501-371-0076) is the logical place to start your visit. The center is in Curran Hall, a residence built in 1842.

Housed in the 1840-vintage former arsenal, the **McArthur Museum of Arkansas Military History** (503 East 9th St.; 501-376-4597) honors Gen. Douglas McArthur, who was born in Little Rock.

Mount Holly Cemetery (1200 South Broadway St.) dates to 1843 and is often referred to as Arkansas's Westminster Abbey. Covering four square blocks, the cemetery is the final resting place of a broad cross section of individuals, including early American Indians, enslaved people, military figures (including four Confederate generals), politicians (including eleven former governors), writers, poets, and others. A brochure for a self-guided tour of the cemetery is available online, at the cemetery office, and elsewhere.

The **Little Rock National Cemetery** (2523 Springer Blvd.; 479-783-5345) has Union and Confederate graves as well as those of other military veterans.

The city's once-rowdy red-light district was located where **Little Rock's Riverfront Park** (400 President Clinton Ave.) stretches eleven blocks along the south bank of the Arkansas River and now covers thirty-three acres. The park has a history pavilion that tells the riverfront's story.

Old Statehouse Museum (300 West Markham St.; 501-324-9685) is located in a Greek Revival structure built in 1833 that served as Arkansas's capitol until 1911. After extensive remodeling, the former statehouse opened to the public as a museum in the early 1950s. With permanent and temporary exhibits, its extensive collection includes material related to the old Arkansas prison. (The current state capitol stands on the original site of the prison.)

Four of Arkansas's oldest buildings, dating to the 1820s and 1830s, stood in disrepair in the capital city until a woman named Louise Loughborough spearheaded an effort in 1939 to get state funding for the restoration of the structures. That was the beginning of the **Historic Arkansas Museum** (200 East 3rd St.; 501-324-9621), which opened in the summer of 1941. Much expanded in the 1970s, the museum's permanent and temporary exhibits focus on Arkansas's frontier history. Among the museum's holdings is a large Bowie knife collection.

Bronco Billy Rode Again and Again

On March 21, 1880, at their home in Little Rock, a Jewish traveling salesman named Henry Aronson and his wife Ester became parents of a boy they named Gilbert Maxwell. Three years later, the family moved to Pine Bluff, Arkansas, where young Gilbert Maxwell grew up. At twenty, Aronson—who went by Max—left Arkansas for New York. He worked as a photographer's assistant and a model before becoming a vaudeville performer. His big break came in 1903 when he got a part in a film made by Edwin S. Porter, *The Great Train Robbery*. In that now-classic silent movie, Aronson adopted G.M. Anderson as his stage name.

Aronson moved to Chicago in 1907 and, with booking agent George K. Spoor, started Essanay Studios. In addition to getting married in 1908, Aronson began producing Westerns in which he starred as Bronco Billy. By 1915 he had appeared in or directed 375 silent Westerns, many featuring the exploits of Bronco Billy. He moved to California in 1912 and after selling his company in 1916, spent the rest of his life there. In 1958 he received an honorary Oscar for his role in the development of the movie industry. The old movie buckaroo died at age ninety in Pasadena in 1971.

The house at 713 Center Street where Aronson was born no longer stands, but in 2018 the Jewish American Society for Historical Preservation dedicated a historical marker near the site summarizing his life and career. The marker stands in front of the First United Methodist Church (723 Center St.).

LONOKE (LONOKE COUNTY)

Lonoke was not named for someone named Lonoke. It was named for a tree, specifically, a lone oak that stood prominently at the future townsite east of Little Rock. By 1867 the name of the community had evolved from Lone Oak to Loneoak to Lonoak to Lonoke. That name endured, though the lone oak was cut down in 1900. The town grew as a county seat and railroad stop and in the late nineteenth century became the venue for a bloody feud.

On April 19, 1898, a would-be assassin shot and wounded C.E. "Charley" Booe (1865–1898) as he emerged from his law office in England, a town in Lonoke County. Booe did not see his attacker but publicly accused Robert Eagle. His father, William K. Booe (1836–1898), agreed with his son that it must have been Eagle, making it known that he intended to permanently rid the county of Robert Eagle and all the other Eagle men. Charley's older brother Will (1862–1898) vowed to help in the endeavor. The elder Booe went to the storehouse in England owned by Robert Eagle, still making no secret of his intention to avenge his son's shooting. Eagle escaped out the back door and hastened to Lonoke, fifteen miles south of England, to report what had happened. Family patriarch William H. Eagle (1835–1906) offered to pay Charley Booe's expenses for a year if he would move to Texas, and friends of both families tried to diffuse the situation, but the Booes declared they would have their revenge.

The Booe family did not have the best of reputations. A prominent grocer (whose store stood next door to a store owned by the Eagles), William K. Booe always put money in the collection plate at church. But everyone in the county knew he and his boys never hesitated to pull a trigger if they believed someone had wronged them. As a young man, William Sr. had shot and wounded two men owing him money. On another occasion, son Will had done the same thing to someone else. And while William and Will had only wounded their victims, Charley had earlier killed a thirteen-year-old boy and then fled to Texas before returning and settling in Arkansas. When Charley finally faced trial for murder, it was William Eagle, the father of the man he now accused of ambushing him, who successfully defended him in court.

The Eagles, on the other hand, were a respected family. William Eagle, a wealthy lawyer and landowner, had served as a colonel in the Confederate army. His brother James had been governor of Arkansas.

Seeing no prospect of peace, the younger Eagle men armed themselves. Rather than waiting for the Booes to make a move, they decided on preemptive action. Hearing on April 25 that William Booe and his two boys (Charley had not been seriously wounded) were headed to Lonoke, five Eagles and one in-law strode to the train station to await their arrival. They watched in hiding as the Booes—all well-armed—alighted from one of the coaches and headed south from the depot down Center Street. As the Booes approached Ruble's Store, the Eagles opened fire. When the gun smoke dissipated, all three Booes lay dead.

Authorities promptly arrested Robert Eagle, Joseph P. Eagle (1862–1935), Joseph E. Eagle (1848–1899), Dave B. Eagle (1870–1927), Miles Henry Eagle (1850–1922), and brother-in-law Robert S. Daughtry. Free on $1,000 bonds they soon were indicted for second-degree murder. Before the case came up on the docket, the local judge recused himself. With a visiting judge presiding at the trial, attorney Joe T. Robinson (who went on to a noted career) argued that Charley Booe was an outlaw and that the Booes had threatened the "extinction" of the Eagles. The jury agreed with Robinson's self-defense argument and acquitted the six men.

Charley, his brother Will, and their father William are buried in **Lonoke Cemetery** (State Highway 89 at Kirk Avenue). Many members of the Eagle family lie in the same cemetery, including family patriarch William and feud participants Dave, Joseph E., Joseph P., and Miles.

Lonoke County Museum (215 Southeast Front St.; 501-676-6750) tells the county's story.

MALVERN (HOT SPRING COUNTY)

Malvern, named for Malvern Hill, Virginia, began as a railroad town in 1870 when the Cairo and Fulton Railroad built through that part of the state. Eight years later, Malvern became the county seat. For fifteen years, Malvern benefited economically from being the nearest railroad depot to the resort town of Hot Springs. From Malvern, people who wanted to enjoy Hot Springs mineral waters traveled the rest of the way—twenty-five miles over a rough road—by stagecoach.

Who Was That Masked Man?

The heavy traffic between Malvern and Hot Springs was good for business—and outlaws. On January 15, 1874, four masked horsemen intercepted a stagecoach with fourteen passengers on

57

their way to Hot Springs. At gunpoint, one of the road agents ordered everyone to alight from the stage and hand over their money and any valuables. Collecting coin, cash, and gold watches, the robbers then slit the mail pouches and tore open any registered letters they found.

Before they left, the man who seemed to be the leader of the gang asked if any of the male passengers had fought for the South during the late war. One man answered yes, but the outlaw wanted more proof, asking the man's rank and outfit. Finally satisfied that the man had served in the Confederate army, the gunman returned that passenger's money and watch.

The gang leader's obvious Southern sympathies and his prankish nature (he had jokingly threatened to shoot a couple of the other male passengers) gave rise to the belief that he was Jesse James. No one ever came up with proof that the stagecoach heist actually was the work of the James gang, but whoever pulled it off, they were never captured.

Visitors can learn more about the supposed Jesse James holdup and the rest of the county's history at the **Hot Spring County Museum** (302 East 3rd St.; 501-337-4775). Opened in 1981, the museum occupies the 1890-vintage **Jacob and Agnus Boyle House**.

NEWPORT (JACKSON COUNTY)

At a crossing of the White River long used by American Indians, Newport developed before the Civil War as a riverboat landing, but it was not incorporated until 1875. Later, steamboat traffic waned when Newport gained a railroad connection.

End of the Line for Conductor McNally

A fifty-two-year-old Irishman, **William P. McNally** had been a conductor on the Poplar Bluff, Missouri, to Little Rock, Arkansas, run of the St. Louis, Iron Mountain and Southern Railway since the early 1880s. Well regarded by colleagues and passengers, he was close to retiring, but he never got that gold watch. On the night of November 3, 1893, the seven cars of the Iron Mountain's Train Number 51 pulled onto a siding at the depot in Olyphant, a small town in Jackson County, to drop off mail and allow passage of the faster *Cannonball Express*. Of the three hundred passengers, many were well-to-do individuals on their way home from the Chicago World's Fair. Suddenly, amid a flurry of gunshots, bandits rushed the train. Borrowing a pistol from one of the passengers, McNally rushed from the train to confront the robbers. The conductor got off several shots—all missing—before one of the bandits ended that railroad man's life with a .30-30 rifle slug in the chest. Within twenty minutes, the outlaws collected $6,000 from the express car and relieved most of the passengers of their cash and jewelry.

One of Arkansas's most intensive manhunts followed, but it wasn't until December that the four principal actors were arrested. The following January, suspects Tom Brady, Jim Wyrick, and Albert Mansker went to trial. Following a month-long proceeding, they were found guilty of murder and sentenced to hang. The fourth defendant, George Padgett, testified against his three associates and was tried separately. He received a life sentence for his cooperation. The other three holdup men were hanged outside the Newport city jail April 6, 1894. The Jackson County holdup proved to be Arkansas's last train robbery and the triple execution was the final legal mass hanging in US history.

The defendants were tried in the then-new **Jackson County Courthouse** (208 Main St.), built in 1872. A three-story, late Victorian red brick building with a distinctive square clock tower rising another three stories, the courthouse was used for the next twenty years. The building was listed on the National Register of Historic Places in 1976.

In the former county seat of Jacksonport, the old courthouse—now in **Jacksonport State Park** (111 Avenue St.; 870-523-2143)—houses a museum that has an exhibit on the train robbery, including a stirrup from the saddle John Wyrick used in the robbery.

The restored 1902 **Iron Mountain Depot** (401 Front St.) displays an assortment of vintage railroad items along with an exhibit on the 1893 holdup.

Former sheriff **James Martin Hobgood** (1860–1905), who was in on the arrest of the suspects and presided over their hanging, is buried in **Newport's Walnut Grove Cemetery** (North Magnolia and Daugherty Streets). The three executed men are believed to have been buried in the Hot Springs vicinity, but the location of their graves has been forgotten. McNally's burial location also is unknown.

PARAGOULD (GREENE COUNTY)

Despite being part of a culture that did not always shy away from resolving differences with a pistol or a sharp-bladed Arkansas "toothpick," early Arkansas residents apparently did not mind the occasional compromise. After all, there are the towns called Arkadelphia and Texarkana. When two vigorously competing railroads—one controlled by J. W. Paramore, the other by Jay Gould—were laying track across the state on their way to Texas markets, they intersected in Greene County. That made for an excellent townsite, which was platted in 1881. But the railroads could not agree on a name for the community. Finally, someone suggested that the new town honor both men, hence Paragould.

By the early 1900s, the West had largely been pacified, but occasional instances of violence reminiscent of the not-so-distant frontier days still occurred. On December 28, 1909, James Henry Trammell shot and mortally wounded Charles Gragg inside the **Elk Café** (203 South Pruitt St.). Since the shooting took place in front of witnesses, the case was no whodunit. But Trammell did not stick around for his day in court. He jumped out a back window before officers arrived. Though hunted by a posse following bloodhounds, he remained on the lam for two years before getting arrested in California and being returned to Arkansas. Again, that was not all that unusual, but what happened next was. He broke out of the Greene County Jail and was never again seen in Paragould. More than a century passed before Old West historian Erik Wright started researching the case and solved the mystery. Wright found that after Trammell escaped jail, he made it back to California. This time, however, he kept going—all the way to kangaroo country in Australia. Wright tracked down an elderly Aussie who was Trammell's grandson. The descendant told Wright that his down under family had known that their relative left the US because he was in trouble, they just didn't know how much trouble until Wright told the surprised grandson the full story. The suspected killer lived to be eighty-six, dying in 1966. It's no longer a café, but the privately-owned building where the shooting took place still stands.

PINE BLUFF (JEFFERSON COUNTY)

What would become Pine Bluff began as a fur trading post established in 1819 by Joseph Bonne on a high, wooded bluff looking down on the Arkansas River. After the signing of a treaty in which the local Quapaw people ceded their land to the US in 1824, other settlers arrived and built cabins in the vicinity and the town grew from there. Jefferson County was formed in 1829 and the Pine Bluff community became county seat in 1832. By the beginning of the Civil War the town had developed into a busy riverport and transportation crossroads.

"Bully for Wild Bill!"

During the war, a young Union soldier named James Butler Hickok had several close calls in and around Pine Bluff. On more than one occasion, a Confederate bullet could have denied American popular culture one of its most famous gunslingers—Wild Bill Hickok.

In 1863, well aware that the usual fate of captured spies was execution, with the full knowledge of Gen. Samuel Curtis of the Eighth Missouri State Militia, Hickok infiltrated a company of mounted Confederates. He knew of a Rebel soldier named Barnes who had been killed in the Battle of Pea Ridge near Fayetteville, Arkansas, and in volunteering his services to the Rebel unit, he posed as the dead man's brother. The ruse worked and Hickok spent five months under cover, collecting valuable military intelligence.

After learning which Confederate regiments were operating in Arkansas, their strength, and even how much artillery they had, Hickok decided it was time to "desert" the Confederacy and get the information back to his commander. "'Twas time for me to go," he told an interviewer after the war, "but it wasn't easy to git out, for the river was close picketed on both sides."

Finally, he developed a plan. A Rebel sergeant claimed he couldn't be beat in a fist fight and Hickok said he'd take him on. But he said the bout should take place on the nearby Arkansas River's edge so the Yankees who held the ground on the other side could see how tough their adversaries were. Unfortunately for Hickok, as the proceedings were about to get under way, some Union soldier recognized Hickok and yelled, "Bully for Wild Bill!" That wouldn't have been a problem except for the fact that the Rebels heard it.

Hickok told what happened next: "Then the sargent suspicioned me, for he turned on me and growled, 'By God, I believe yer a Yank!' And he at onst drew his revolver; but he was too late, for the minute he drew his pistol I put a ball through him."

With bullets buzzing past him, Hickok rode his horse into the river and made it to the other side.

Learn about the history of the area at the **Pine Bluff-Jefferson County Historical Museum** (201 East 4th Ave.; 870-541-5402). The museum occupies the 1906 Union Station, a structure listed on the National Register of Historic Places. The city has fifty-seven additional structures on the register, including the **1850 Dexter Harding House** (110 North Pine St.; 870-536-8742), which houses the visitor information center.

POTTSVILLE (POPE COUNTY)

Kirkbride Potts settled in 1828 on recently vacated Cherokee land near where Galla Creek flowed into the Arkansas River and built a two-level cabin for his family. Potts eventually acquired 650 acres in the vicinity, land through which passed the well-traveled military road from Missouri to Fort Smith, Arkansas. Learning of the gold discovery in California, Potts left his wife and children behind and headed west to strike it rich. He did not find gold, but while in California he realized he could make gold another way—by selling beef to miners. After that, he put together two cattle drives from Arkansas to the gold fields. The trips were hard and dangerous, but he made a handsome profit, and in 1850, with enslaved labor, he began building a much more substantial home for his family.

When the Butterfield Overland Mail began using the military road in 1857, Potts's two-and-a-half-story house became a stagecoach stop known as Potts Inn. Potts and his wife rented beds for the night (they had room for up to thirty-two guests) and served meals. Following Potts's death in 1879, his son asked that the town that had grown around the inn be named for his father, which it was.

Potts's descendants continued to live in the antebellum house until 1970, when they sold it to Pope County. The home was then renovated and opened as the **Potts Inn Museum** (15 East Ash St.; 479-968-8369), operated by the Pope County Historical Foundation. Since then, five historic log structures have been moved to the property for use as exhibit space.

ROGERS (BENTON COUNTY)

Originally a stagecoach stop on the Old Wire Road (the one-time Indian trail along which extended the first telegraph line connecting St. Louis with Fort Smith, Arkansas) known as Callahan Spring, this area accommodated a construction camp when the St. Louis and San Francisco Railroad began building across northwestern Arkansas in 1881. Once trains began rolling through, the town that developed there was named Rogers after C.W. Rogers, vice president and general manager of the Frisco, as the rail line was popularly known.

The Other Gun That Won the West

The six-shot revolver developed by Samuel Colt is known as the gun that won the West, as are the Henry, Sharps, and Winchester rifles, but arguably the title should go to a cutting-edge weapon that traveled with the 1803–1806 Lewis and Clark Expedition—an air gun.

First manufactured in Italy in 1780, the **Girandoni air rifle** featured a detachable, high-pressure flask that constituted the stock of the weapon. Four feet long and weighing ten pounds, the hand-pumped pneumatic weapon was capable of propelling a .46-caliber lead ball at a thousand feet per second, a velocity sufficient for the bullet to punch through a one-inch plank at one hundred yards. Even some modern firearms are not that powerful. And unlike the flintlock rifles of the era, the air rifle could fire up to forty rounds—quickly—before the reservoir had to be recharged.

Needless to say, when they saw it demonstrated, the American Indians encountered by the Corps of Discovery along the way quickly grasped the weapon's awesome capability. What they didn't know was that the soldiers only had one of the high-tech rifles then known as Wind Guns.

What does this have to do with Rogers, Arkansas? Since 1958, the city has been the home of Daisy Outdoor Products, makers since 1888 of Daisy air rifles. In a remodeled former bank built in 1906 is the **Daisy Airgun Museum** (202 West Walnut St.; 479-986-6873), a venue dedicated to the history of pneumatic rifles and pistols. Two display cases exhibit various air guns made between 1770 and 1820, including a vintage weapon similar to the one carried by the Lewis and Clark party. Also displayed at the museum are the various Daisy BB gun replicas of the famed Colt Peacemaker and Winchester Model 1894 lever-action .30-30 rifle. For visitors looking for a good selfie shot, in January 2021

> the manufacturer erected outside the museum a twenty-five-foot-tall sculpture of a Daisy BB gun, leaning against the building.

The **Rogers Historical Museum** (322 South 2nd St.) focuses on the city's history.

SAINT PAUL (MADISON COUNTY)

Founded in 1887 in northwest Arkansas when a rail line came through the county, Saint Paul is only a small town but one of the West's more interesting characters was born in Madison County and he's buried here.

"Texas Jack" Died with His Boots Off

His long silver-gray hair cascading from beneath a flat-brimmed black cowboy hat, the sidewalk evangelist worked the streets of Tulsa, Oklahoma, warning all who would listen against a life of crime. He knew whereof he spoke.

Born in Madison County, Arkansas, in 1862, Nathaniel Jack Reed would become far better known as Texas Jack. During the 1880s and '90s, he was one of the Wild West's most-wanted outlaws. Across Texas, Oklahoma, and in the Rockies, Reed and his fellow bandits robbed stagecoaches, trains, and banks. In helping himself to others' money, he had not been at all reluctant to shoot. Finally captured after deputy US marshals wounded him in a shootout, Reed cut a deal with Federal Judge Isaac Parker at Fort Smith and flipped on his cohorts in exchange for a five-year sentence. Paroled in 1896 after serving one year, Reed announced his reformation and took to preaching on street corners.

Texas Jack also traveled in Wild West shows, published a memoir in 1936 called *The Life of Texas Jack*, and clearly enjoyed the attention he received as a reformed outlaw. He exaggerated his claims, but no one could argue he wasn't colorful. He died of old age in 1950, bitter to the end that Hollywood never produced a movie based on his life. Finally, in 2016, such a film came out, *Stagecoach: The Texas Jack Story*. The movie flopped at the box office.

Under a ground-level granite marker bearing only his name and dates of birth and death, Texas Jack lies in **Riverside Cemetery**, also known as Saint Paul Cemetery (GPS coordinates: N35° 49.78', W93° 45.13'). His long-out-of-print book is a highly sought collectible.

The **Shiloh Museum of Ozark History** (118 West Johnson Ave., Springdale; 479-750-8165) covers the rich history of northwest Arkansas.

SILOAM SPRINGS (BENTON COUNTY)

On the Oklahoma border in the northwest corner of Arkansas, settlement of the area that would become Siloam Springs began with a trading post established in the mid-1840s on Sager Creek. First known as Hico Trading Post, by 1855 it was just called Hico. After the Civil War, John Hargrove bought farmland in the area that included the creek named for the area's first settler, Simon Sager.

In 1880, hoping a mineral spring in the area could become a destination for health-seekers, Hargrove had a townsite platted on his land and named the new community Siloam Springs. The place fell a bit short of becoming another Hot Springs, but it grew and soon eclipsed Hico.

Hornswoggled by Belle Starr

The notorious Belle Starr spent some time in Siloam Springs, which was just across from Oklahoma and not too far from Fort Smith. Her first husband (Jim Reed) was born here, and Belle's daughter Pearl (who went on to become a noted Fort Smith madam) gave birth to an illegitimate daughter here.

Legend has it that in 1884, Belle challenged John Hargrove to a horse race (in addition to building the town, Hargrove also raised thoroughbred horses). One of his horses, a black stallion, never lost a race. Consequently, the breeder made good money wagering on the steed. Whether she raised them or stole them, Belle Starr also appreciated fine horse flesh.

Hargrove readily accepted and a crowd of a thousand showed up to watch the match. Supposedly, Belle told the American Indian who'd be riding her horse to pace the animal so it would only beat Hargrove's horse by a neck. She figured Hargrove would demand a rematch and bet even more heavily on his horse. That's purportedly what happened. Only the second time, Belle's jockey rode to win, and did. Hargrove lost so much money, the story goes, that he ended up committing suicide. However he departed this world, his death indeed occurred in 1884—August 8 to be exact. That was a Friday, a good day for a horse race.

Hargrave is buried in **Hico Cemetery** (East Tahlequah and North Hill Streets).

Learn about the history and culture of the area at the **Siloam Springs Museum** (112 North Maxwell St.; 479-524-4011).

TEXARKANA (MILLER COUNTY)

The state-line city of Texarkana is a different sort of place. For one thing, as simple as the logic behind its name appears ("Tex" for Texas, "ark" for Arkansas and "ana" for Louisiana), no one has yet determined who first thought of it. The general belief, whichever of a half-dozen stories is true, is that the advent of the word "Texarkana" long preceded the founding of the community. The second thing that makes Texarkana unusual is that it has a counterpart in Texas by the same name. And though they're only separated by a street, the two cities haven't always gotten along.

While occupation of the area that eventually became Texarkana goes back much further, the town is an offspring of the railroad. In the early 1870s, the Texas and Pacific Railroad was laying track north-eastward as the Cairo and Illinois moved southwest through Missouri toward Arkansas. Once the two roads connected, the Texas and Pacific would concentrate on heading westward. But there were legal and cost issues involved with the Cairo and Illinois (which eventually became the Missouri Pacific Railroad) entering Texas to join the Texas and Pacific. To get around that, the two companies decided to meet at the Texas border.

The Texas and Pacific acquired and sold town lots on the Texas side, the Illinois company did the same on the Arkansas side. Lot sales began in Texarkana, Texas, in December 1873, followed in January 1874 by Texarkana, Arkansas. When the two Texarkanas achieved through-rail service (eventually it gained three other railroads), the resulting boom brought prosperity and classic Wild West–style lawlessness. While that happened all over the West, outlaws had it even easier in one or the other of the Texarkanas because all they had to do to avoid local officers was cross the street to the other state.

Gambling was rampant in Texarkana for years, which makes it no surprise that one of the city's oldest houses is said to have been funded with builder James H. Draughon's poker winnings. Supposedly, the lumberman won the pot with an ace-high hand. Accordingly, the Italianate Victorian house he purchased is known as the **Ace of Clubs House** (420 Pine St.). Not only that, with twenty-two sides, three octagonal wings, and one rectangular wing, it is configured like the club suite. Built in 1885, the house was acquired by the Texarkana Museum System, renovated, and opened as a museum in 1988.

The **Museum of Regional History** (219 State Line Ave.; 903-793-4831) occupies the twin city's oldest brick structure, built in 1879. Opened in 1971, the museum covers all aspects of the area's history, from the original Caddoan people followed by French and Spanish explorers through the wild and wooly boom era to the twentieth century.

VAN BUREN (CRAWFORD COUNTY)

The first settlers came to this area on the east bank of the Arkansas River just below the Ozark's Boston Mountains in 1818. John Drennen and brother-in-law David Thompson later paid $11,000 for acreage along the river and in 1836 laid out a townsite named for Secretary of State (and future president) Martin Van Buren. Riverboats brought people and goods to Van Buren and the port city, incorporated in 1845, soon served as a waypoint for California-bound gold seekers. In 1857 Van Buren became a stagecoach stop on the Butterfield Overland Mail route.

A historical marker explaining the 1857–1861 **Butterfield Overland Mail**, which traveled through town along Main Street, stands on the grounds of the Crawford County Courthouse (300 Main St.).

Located in the old Frisco Railroad depot, the **River Valley Museum** (813 Main St.; 800-332-5889) has exhibits relating to the city's history.

The **Van Buren Visitor Center**, also located in the 1901-vintage depot, provides a self-guided walking tour pointing out ten historic downtown buildings.

Operated by the University of Arkansas at Fort Smith, the **Drennan-Scott Historic Site** (321 North 3rd St.) features John Drennan's restored one-story log and clapboard home. He built it in 1836, the year Arkansas became a state. Exhibits in the historic site's visitor center tell the story of Drennan, his house, and the city he founded. The structure was listed on the National Register status in 1971.

Just Another Horse Thief

On March 28, 1871, three young men stole two horses near Fort Gibson in the Cherokee Nation. The crime was reported to deputy US Marshal Jacob Owens, who swore out a complaint alleging that the suspects did "feloniously, willfully steal take and carry away" a pair of horses valued at $100 each. The US commissioner for the Western District of Arkansas, the federal court then based in Van Buren, issued arrest warrants for the three men and Deputy Owens led a posse to find them. The posse trailed the suspects for two hundred miles before arresting them just south of the Kansas border. The men were taken to Van Buren where, unable to make their $500 bonds, they were locked up in the Crawford County jail. Their names were **Ed Kennedy**, **John Shown**, and **Wyatt Earp**, former Lamar, Missouri, constable and future participant in what would come to be called the Gunfight at the OK Corral.

The following month seven men escaped the jail by breaking through its roof. Two of them were Shown and Earp. Kennedy, who chose to stay behind, was later tried and acquitted. Neither the owner of the horses nor the principal witness appeared for the proceeding, so more than likely Earp and Shown would have walked had they stayed around.

The jail Earp and Shown escaped from was razed to make room for a new jail built in 1892 and used until 1940. That two-story brick structure still stands. At the time of the escape, the Western District of Arkansas was in the process of moving to Fort Smith from Van Buren, where the court shared usage of the **Crawford County Courthouse**. The two-story brick Italianate-style structure was built in 1841 and 1842. Fire gutted the building six years later, leaving only the blackened walls still standing. But the county rebuilt the courthouse to its original specifications. The building at 317 Main Street is still in use, the oldest operating courthouse west of the Mississippi.

WASHINGTON (HEMPSTEAD COUNTY)

A steamboat landing on the Red River and a stopping place on the old trail between St. Louis, Missouri, and Fulton, Arkansas, Washington was founded February 22, 1824—George Washington's birthday. In the 1830s and 1840s, Cherokee and Choctaw Indians passed through Washington on their way to new land in what would become Oklahoma, a forced passage that came to be known as the Trail of Tears. At the same time, Washington was the gateway to early Texas. Stephen F. Austin, Sam Houston, James Bowie, David Crockett, and hundreds of others came through the bustling, rowdy town.

A Different Kind of Knife

If the Colt six-shooter won the West, the blade that sliced its way into Western lore was the Bowie knife. Washington blacksmith James Black is said to have made the prototype of the distinctive, and deadly, weapon per James Bowie's specifications. But most histories of the knife have it being developed in Louisiana by Rezin Bowie, James's brother. Whoever developed the knife, Black can definitely be credited with perfecting the so-called Arkansas Toothpick, a long-bladed dirk that also became a Wild West standard. What state should get the credit for the Bowie knife aside, an assortment of vintage Bowie knives are displayed in the **B. W. Edwards Weapons Museum** (103 Franklin St.; 870-983-2684). The former bank houses a collection of six hundred vintage firearms and bladed weapons gathered by the museum's namesake, who willed his collection to the state.

When the US and Mexico went to war in 1846, Washington was a gathering place for volunteer soldiers from Arkansas and other states headed to Texas.

Missed by the railroad in the 1870s and later losing its county seat status, Washington faded into decline. Fortunately, several score of its historic nineteenth-century structures have survived. The Pioneer Washington Restoration Foundation began rehabilitating the town's historic buildings in 1958 and **Historic Washington State Park** (103 Franklin St.; 870-983-2684) opened in 1974. The town is also a National Register of Historic Places site.

MISSOURI

Arrow Rock (Saline County)

For thousands of years before Euro-American settlement began in Missouri, American Indians fashioned projectile points from flint they collected from the limestone bluffs rising above the Missouri River in what is now Saline County. When the Lewis and Clark Expedition passed through in the summer of 1804, Clark noted the geologic feature and the prairie above it, an area he referred to as "Prairie of Arrows." In the early 1820s, travelers journeying west to New Mexico on the newly blazed Santa Fe Trail crossed the river at this point, and by 1829 the town of Arrow Rock had become a significant waypoint and riverboat landing. Later, Arrow Rock saw waves of Missouri volunteers marching through on their way to Santa Fe to take part in the 1846–1848 Mexican War. Arrow Rock's potential for further growth was stunted after the Civil War when riverboat traffic declined as railroads began to expand across the West.

Covering 167 acres, the **Arrow Rock Historic Site** (39521 Visitor Center Dr.; 660-837-3330) includes thirty-eight old buildings, among them the 1834 **J. Huston Tavern** (305 Main St.; 660-837-3200)—the oldest continuously operating restaurant west of the Mississippi. The visitor center in this National Historic District features an interpretive video and exhibits detailing the long history of the area.

Firearms for the Frontier

John P. Sites Jr. began gunsmithing in Arrow Rock in 1844. Having learned the trade from his father, he repaired firearms and converted old flintlock rifles into percussion lock rifles for travelers embarking on the Santa Fe Trail and for local customers. He also manufactured his own brand of rifle for frontier self-protection, hunting, and military use. He could neither read nor write but built a successful business and became widely known as a maker of quality firearms. Sites achieved more local recognition when, to the astonishment of his family and friends, he found religion and foreswore both smoking and swearing. After his death in 1904, his longtime shop (built in 1866) became an automotive garage and telephone office. Following an archeological investigation at the site in the late 1960s, the small, two-story brick building was restored. **The John P. Sites Gunshop** (southwest corner of 5th and High Streets) is the only known restoration of a vintage gun shop on its original location in the nation. Sites-made rifles have been found in every western state, three are on display at the vintage gun shop.

BOONVILLE (COOPER COUNTY)

Famed frontiersman Daniel Boone's two sons, Daniel Morgan and Nathan, began a commercial operation at a salt lick at this point on the Missouri River in 1805. Salt being an important commodity on the frontier, the mineral source began attracting settlers to the area. First known as Boone's Lick, when the town was platted in 1817, the "Lick" was dropped and "ville" added. Given its status as a river port, and with the Santa Fe Trail passing nearby, Boonville became an important waypoint for westward-bound travelers. Following the Civil War, the town developed as a trade center.

Cooper County has more than four hundred buildings listed on the National Register of Historic Places, the majority in Boonville. Opened in 2019, the **River, Rails and Trails Museum** (100 East Spring St.; 660-882-3967) tells Boonville's story. The museum is part of the visitor center, where information on the town's historic properties is available.

The original two-story **Cooper County jail** (614 East Morgan St.; 660-882-7977) was built by enslaved workers who quarried two-and-a-half-foot-thick limestone blocks to create the building in 1848. The county certainly got its money's worth out of the lockup, which cost $6,000. It continued in use for the next 130 years, finally replaced by a new facility in 1978. When first opened, and for years afterward, the original jail consisted of only two large rooms, upstairs and down. Prisoners were shackled to round rings bolted into the walls. In 1871, the county did away with the old "bullpen" concept and installed more traditional cell blocks. Thrifty county officials pressed inmates into duty as laborers on the modernization project. The same year, the county also approved construction of a three-room residence for the sheriff. Not long after, a second story was added along with a kitchen at the rear of the first floor.

The final addition to the jail came in 1878 when the county put up a frame barn near the original structure. During the horseback era, sheriffs kept horses stabled in the barn should the necessity for a posse arise. The barn also enabled sheriffs to be somewhat discrete when required to hang a convicted felon. The last execution took place in the barn in 1930.

Jesse James's older brother Frank briefly cooled his heels in the jail in the spring of 1884. Sheriff John Rogers booked him on April 24 on an arrest warrant issued for an 1876 train robbery. James's sympathizers quickly raised money for his bond. Due to lack of evidence, the case was later dismissed.

Tours of the old jail are offered by the **Friends of Historic Boonville**.

BRANSON (TANEY COUNTY)

Shepherd of the Hills Freeway (State Highway 248) carries tourists and locals through this internationally known, family-friendly entertainment town. The thoroughfare's name evokes a pastoral image entirely fitting for the scenic Ozarks. But in Taney and neighboring Christian County, the name has nothing to do with the rolling, timbered hills, or religiosity, except perhaps the opposite of the latter.

The local significance of the name comes from a novel, a work of fiction based on one of the Wild West's more vicious reigns of terror—the vigilantism associated with an 1880s "law and order" cabal known as the **Bald Knobbers**. That the Bald Knobbers—night riders who wore homemade masks with horns that made them look like devils—came to be linked with such a peaceful sounding name as Shepherd of the Hills can be laid to the work of Harold Bell Wright, an early twentieth-century writer. One of his best-selling novels, published in 1907, was *Shepherd of the Hills*. In the book, a peace-loving preacher named Daniel Howitt opposes the leader of the Bald Knobbers, the very violent Wash Gibbs. Four movies have been based on Wright's novel, and from 1960 to 2017, Branson visitors could attend a play named for and inspired by the novel.

While the stage production based on the nineteenth-century vigilantism is no more, since 1959 a local family of entertainers—calling themselves the Baldknobbers—have put on a country music and comedy variety show in Branson.

There was nothing funny about the real Bald Knobbers, however. What began as an effort to rid the area of evildoers metastasized into evil itself. People adjudged as sinners, from suspected adulterers to Southern sympathizers to run-of-the-mill thieves, were whipped and ordered to leave the county on penalty of death. Worse offenders, real or imagined, ended up shot dead or dangling from trees.

As the reign of terror worsened, an anti-vigilante group formed to rid the area of the Bald Knobbers. Realizing they needed to cut the head off the snake, the group orchestrated the assassination of Nathaniel N. Kinney (1843–1888), founder and leader of the Bald Knobbers. That, of course, only fueled more violence.

Finally the state stepped in, sending in militiamen to round up the so wrongly righteous. Eighty members of the Christian County Bald Knobbers were arrested. Of those, four were found guilty of murder and sentenced to hang. One managed to escape from jail, but the other three were hanged in the spring of 1889. However, the executions were mishandled. The ropes were too long and when the trap door sprang, the three condemned men fell to their feet still in relatively good health and had to be hanged a second time.

The botched hangings marked the end of the worst of the violence, but what had evolved into a feud simmered for years.

In 2009 the Christian County Historical Society erected an engraved stone marker (101 North 2nd St.) in Ozark on the courthouse lawn at the site of the botched hangings. One side summarizes the Bald Knobbers' story while the other side features a chilling rendition of the Bald Knobber mask. Beneath are words that would do for scores of historical sites across the West:

This marker is not to commemorate the violent acts resulting in many deaths, including those hanged here. It has been erected so that we will remember what happened, so it does not happen again. We would like to forget this part of our past but must not.

At nearby Forsyth, the county seat, the **White River Valley Historical Society Museum** (297 Main St.; 417-546-2210) has an exhibit on the Bald Knobbers as well as research material and books related to the lawless period.

Nathaniel Kinney, the man who organized the Bald Knobbers, is buried in **Forsyth Cemetery** (479 Coy Blvd.), two miles from town just past Forsyth School. Also buried there is Margaret Carriger Kinney (1841–1891), wife of the vigilante leader, and Bald Knobber Charles H. Groom (1861–1945).

Barton Yell Everett (1848–1918), another key Bald Knobber figure, lies in Taney County's **Ragsdale Cemetery**, off Caney Road, southeast of Taneyville (GPS coordinates: N36° 42.98', W93° 05.90').

In Ridgedale, ten miles south of Branson, the **Ancient Ozarks Natural History Museum** (150 Top of the Rock Rd.; 800-255-6343) features founder Johnny Morris's collection of Western art and Old West artifacts. While the museum does cover the area's natural history, its name is something of a misnomer because it also has exhibits related to American Indians, the Civil War, and the Old West.

CARTHAGE (JASPER COUNTY)

Carthage was settled along Spring River in 1842. The town was named for the ancient city on the northern coast of Africa and later shared one aspect of that city's history. Just as the Romans destroyed the first Carthage, this Missouri town was put to the torch during the Civil War. Rebuilt in 1866, after the war the town prospered from lead and zinc mining in the area and as an agricultural center.

She Could Play the Piano, Ride ... and Shoot

Myra Maybelle Shirley—later far better known as **Belle Starr**—spent her first sixteen years in or around Carthage. She was born February 5, 1848, on the family farm near the Jasper County community of Medoc. The woman her father, John R. Shirley, married, Elizabeth Hatfield of the infamous Hatfield family that long feuded with the McCoys, was twenty years his junior.

Shirley later sold his rural holdings and moved his family to Carthage, where he was a substantial property owner. Young Myra received a good education at the Carthage Female Academy, where she learned the piano. She also loved the outdoors and became an accomplished horsewoman. One of her childhood friends was Cole Younger, who would eventually team up with Frank and Jesse James. The Shirley family moved to Texas in 1864. Later, Myra became infamously known as Belle Starr, "The Bandit Queen."

The old house in which Starr is said to have been born was restored, expanded, and moved in 1990 from its original location to a collection of vintage buildings assembled and restored by Lowell Davis known as **Red Oak II** (10725 County Loop 122), four miles northeast of Carthage just off old Route 66. Davis grew up in the small Jasper County town of Red Oak, a place that withered after World War II. A successful artist, in 1987 Davis began acquiring and moving old buildings from Red Oak to his farm twenty-three miles away. That was the genesis of Red Oak II.

The Carthage Female Academy, founded in 1855, occupied a brick building in the 700 block of South Main at the northwest corner of Carthage's public square. It was destroyed during the Civil War. The **Carthage Hotel** (which included a saloon and livery stable) stood several doors to the east.

To learn more about the history of the area, visit the **Powers Museum** (617 Oak St.; 417-237-0456), which is devoted to Carthage's history. The **Carthage Convention and Visitors Bureau** (402 South Garrison Ave.; 417-359-8181), has more information on the community.

COLUMBIA (BOONE COUNTY)

The Osage and Missouri Tribes lived in the vicinity of future Columbia during the time of the first French exploration of the area in the 1600s. After the French sold Missouri and most of the rest of the West to the US in 1803, the Lewis and Clark Expedition passed through this area. The first Euro-American settlement here was Smithton, founded in 1819. Insufficient water led to the demise of the community in the spring of 1821 and the roughly twenty settlers relocated to a location they called Columbia. The town, which grew into an educational center, was incorporated in 1826.

The **Boone County History and Culture Center** (3801 Ponderosa St.) includes a county history museum. However, researchers and family historians wanting to learn more about the Wild West, or any other aspect of Missouri's history, should start at the **Center for Missouri Studies** (605 Elm St.; 800-747-6366). The center, located in a building opened in the summer of 2019, houses extensive archival, cartographic, photographic, and newspaper collections as well as rotating exhibits. The center is operated by the Missouri Historical Society, which has branches in Camp Girardeu, Kansas City, Rolla, St. Louis, and Springfield.

GADS HILL (WAYNE COUNTY)

When George Creath founded a town in 1871 along the planned route of the Iron Mountain Railroad in a heavily wooded area of Wayne County, he named it Gads Hill for the rural retreat of novelist Charles Dickens. Three years later, the community had only a few residents, a general store, and a train depot. The hamlet never grew but achieved a place in Wild West history.

As the Iron Mountain Railroad's Number 7 passenger train rolled south on its regular run to Little Rock, Arkansas, the engineer saw someone standing in the track at the small Gads Hill depot—normally just a whistle-stop—waving a red flag. The person with the flag did not look like a railroad man, but a red flag meant danger and the engineer threw the brakes. In this case, while the red flag did not warn of a washout or any other hazard to the train, it did indeed signal danger. It was Saturday, January 31, 1874.

With the train stopped, five men armed with shotguns and six-shooters took all the money in the express car and walked down the aisles in the two passenger cars collecting money and valuables from everyone but working men and ladies. Vicious threats at gunpoint got people to do what the bandits wanted, but no shots were fired.

Before the outlaws rode off with roughly $2,000, their leader handed a handwritten press release to a passenger and told him to make sure the *St. Louis Dispatch* got it. The bandit's name was Jesse James.

The Piedmont Lions Club has a large wooden sign (GPS coordinates: N37° 14.30', W90° 41.84') off State Highway 49 in Gads Hill marking the site of the robbery.

GALLATIN (DAVIESS COUNTY)

Founded in 1837, Gallatin's a small town in the northwestern part of the state, but it looms large in the saga of **Jesse** and **Frank James**. In fact, it arguably is both where the story began and where it ended.

The beginning came during the noon hour on December 7, 1869, when two young men walked into the **Daviess County Savings Bank** and one of them asked for change for a one-hundred-dollar bill. Cashier John W. Sheets (1818–1869) began counting out the money but suddenly one of the men pulled a revolver and shot him twice, once in the chest and once in the forehead. The only other person in the bank at the time was lawyer William A. McDowell, who rushed from the bank to alert townsfolk to the robbery. As he cleared the entrance, one of the robbers shot at him, hitting him in the arm. After collecting some $700, the two bandits emerged from the bank, firing shots into the air to ward off townspeople flocking toward the scene of the crime.

On their way out of town, one of the men's horses spooked and its rider fell off. The other rider came back to pick up his comrade, and as a posse formed to pursue the men, they disappeared into the countryside. Not too far out of town, the robber who'd lost his horse appropriated someone else's horse, saying he could have the steed he'd left behind in Gallatin. That horse was soon identified as having belonged to Jesse James, sufficient proof for the governor to put a bounty on the brothers.

While Jesse and Frank James were suspected of an 1866 bank robbery in Liberty, Missouri, the Gallatin holdup was the first confirmed James gang holdup. As it turned out, the motive of the crime was more than financial. Sheets was not shot to eliminate him as a witness, but because the James brothers wrongly believed him to be Samuel P. Cox. During the Civil War, Cox had led the effort to hunt down Jesse's friend and fellow bushwhacker "Bloody Bill" Anderson.

Six months after his brother was shot and killed by Robert Ford on April 3, 1882, Frank James surrendered to the governor of Missouri. On August 20, 1883, he went on trial in Gallatin for the murder of Sheets, the 1881 train robbery at Winston, Missouri, and the murder of conductor William Westfall in that holdup. Given that James was arguably the most famous American outlaw at the time, so many people wanted to attend the trial that the proceedings had to be held in an opera house on the second floor of the Anderson Building just across the street from the too-small courthouse. The seventeen-day trial ended in James's acquittal.

The small, one-story brick building at the southeast corner of Market and Grand Streets where the robbery occurred was later razed, and a two-story brick structure stands there today. A wooden plaque on the building notes that the holdup and killing occurred at the site. The opera house where the trial occurred also is gone, but a one-story, twentieth-century building now standing at that spot

(116 North Market St.) has a plaque similar to the one marking the robbery site.

Built in 1888, too late for Jesse James, an unusual rotary or "squirrel cage" jail and sheriff's residence constructed by the Pauly Jail Building and Manufacturing Company (see St. Louis, Missouri) stands two blocks west of the Daviess County Courthouse. Listed on the National Register of Historic Places, the **Daviess County Squirrel Cage Jail** (310 West Jackson St.) is an octagonal brick structure with walls three feet thick on a limestone foundation. The sheriff lived in the T-shaped, two-story house connected to the jail by another two-story structure that housed the jail's kitchen and cells for women. Today the old jail accommodates a museum and visitor center operated by the Daviess County Historical Society.

Though the present courthouse was not constructed until 1908, its records include a lawsuit filed in the Common Pleas Court of Daviess County in 1870 against Frank and Jesse James. The only known civil action listing the James brothers as defendants was filed by one Daniel Smoote, who sought $223.50 for a horse, saddle, and bridle stolen as the brothers fled the 1869 robbery. Despite the fame of the James gang, court documents connected to the civil case, as well as other records involving the outlaws, were believed lost or stolen until discovered in the files of the county circuit clerk's office in 2007. The documents were then digitized by the Missouri State Archives and are now available online.

John Sheets, shot in the head during the 1869 robbery, is buried next to his wife in **Lile Cemetery** (West Richardson and Benton Streets). His white marble tombstone is in the second row from the back of the cemetery.

HANNIBAL (MARION COUNTY)

When Moses Bates laid out Hannibal in 1818 on the west bank of the Missouri River, the western half of the North American continent remained largely unexplored, largely unpopulated by Euro-Americans, and almost entirely unexploited. The US did not yet even own all the land between the Missouri and the Pacific. But on November 30, 1835, only seventeen years after Hannibal's founding, a child born roughly forty miles southwest in Florida, Missouri, would help shape the nation's perception of the Wild West. His name was Samuel Langhorne Clemens, later to become far better known as Mark Twain.

Twain's family moved to Hannibal when he was four and that's where he grew up and gained the inspiration for his two classics, *The Adventures of Tom Sawyer* and *The Adventures of Huck Finn*. In 1861 he traveled by stagecoach with his brother to the booming silver mining town of Carson City, Nevada, and spent the following five years in the West. As a newspaper writer in Virginia City, Nevada, and California, he found his literary voice and adopted his soon-to-be-renowned pen name. His experiences in California inspired the short story that first gained him national attention as a writer, "The Celebrated Jumping Frog of Calaveras County." Twain's 1872 book *Roughing It* detailed his Western adventures and helped contribute to the Western myth.

Start your visit to this area at the **Hannibal Convention and Visitors Bureau** (505 North 3rd St.; 573-221-2477). The two-story, 1843-vintage frame house where the Clemens family lived was about to be torn down in 1911 when the forerunner of Hannibal's chamber of commerce saved it and opened it to the public. One of the West's earliest historical preservation efforts led to a succession of improvements, expansions, and additional acquisitions of Mark Twain–related properties that eventually made Hannibal the mecca for the author's admirers. The **Mark Twain Boyhood Home and Museum** (120 North Main St.; 573-221-9010) has been rated as one of the West's top ten museums. For an overview of Twain's life and to get tickets to all the museum's properties, the museum's interpretive center (415 Main St.) is the place to start. Thirty-nine miles southwest of Hannibal is the **Mark Twain Birthplace State Historic Site** (37352 Shrine Rd., Florida; 573-565-3440). Twain was born in a rented, two-room frame cabin and spent the first four years of his life here. The historic structure, listed on the National Register of Historic Places, has been preserved inside a large, modern museum.

HIGGINSVILLE (LAFAYETTE COUNTY)

Founded in 1869, Higginsville was named for Harvey Higgins, owner of the land platted for the townsite.

During the Civil War in Missouri, Kansas, and as far south as North Texas, **William C. Quantrill** led a ruthless band of Confederates known as **Quantrill's Raiders**. Since two of his guerilla riders were Frank and Jesse James, he can also be viewed as the mentor of two of the Wild West's most infamous outlaws.

When Quantrill died on June 6, 1865, of a wound suffered a month earlier in a skirmish with Union soldiers in Kentucky, he was buried in Louisville. Like any mortal, he could only die once, but unlike most departed souls, he—or at least parts of him—have been buried in three different graves. His mother had his remains exhumed in 1887 for reburial in his hometown of Dover, Ohio. By then only a scattering of bones and his skull remained. While most of the remains are believed to have been laid to rest in Ohio, his skull and a few other bones had a much longer "life." The childhood friend who dug up Quantrill's grave in Kentucky on behalf of the guerilla's mother thought he could make some money off his old pal and kept some of the bones to sell. The bones and Quantrill's skull, which his mother had identified because of a chipped tooth he had, ended up as a college fraternity icon until 1942 and later among the artifacts of the Kansas State Historical Society.

Finally, in 1992, the Kansas organization conveyed the remaining bones to the Missouri Sons of Confederate Veterans for burial in Higginsville. The skull was handed over to the Dover Historical Society, which placed it in a plastic ice chest, glued down the lid, and buried it in **Confederate Home Cemetery**, the same cemetery believed to hold the rest of Quantrill's bones. The cemetery is part of the 135-acre **Confederate Memorial State Historic Site** (211 West 1st St.; 660-584-2853). Established in 1891, the **Confederate Soldiers Home of Missouri** operated here until the last old soldier died at the facility in 1950.

INDEPENDENCE (JACKSON COUNTY)

Three of the Old West's most significant and storied overland transportation routes—the Santa Fe, Oregon, and California Trails—all began in or near Independence. Founded in 1827, Independence soon became the primary "jumping-off" place for westward travelers. First came the nine-hundred-mile Santa Fe Trail in 1821, followed in 1843 by the two-thousand-mile Oregon Trail, and, finally, the equally long California Trail born of the great gold rush of 1849.

For years during the heyday of the trails, Independence came to life each spring, the time of year travelers were most likely to start their dangerous journey across two-thirds of the continent. Thousands of emigrants poured into town with their wagons, teams, and other livestock. Here they purchased the supplies they would need as they made their way through unsettled country presided over by the Plains Indians. From 1840 to 1860, an estimated four hundred thousand people traveled one or another of the trails originating here. Of those, one in ten died along the way.

The **Independence Visitors Center** (937 West Walnut St.; 816-836-3466) offers self-guided walking tour guides. West-bound travelers often camped near a large, prolific spring that once flowed only a hundred yards from what is now the **National Frontier Trails Museum** (318 West Pacific Ave.; 816-325-7575). The spring later powered a small gristmill, an early-day enterprise that grew into a large milling company that continued in operation until destroyed by an explosion and fire in 1967. Twenty-two years later, the state of Missouri incorporated a surviving portion of the old mill into a museum building. Now operated by the city of Independence, the center also serves as home for the **Oregon-California Trails Association**.

Independence continued as a transportation hub even after the west-bound trails fell into disuse. Exhibiting nineteenth-century railroad equipment and artifacts, the 1879-vintage **Chicago and Alton Railroad Depot** (511 South Spring St.; 816-325-7955) is a two-story frame building moved to its present site from its original location.

Independence also has the largest free-standing public genealogy library in the US, the **Midwest Genealogy Center** (3440 South Lee's Summit Rd.; 816-252-7728).

Trials and Tribulations of a Pioneer Woman

Life wasn't easy for a woman headed west on the Oregon Trail. To commemorate the grit that it took, in 1990 a six-foot bronze statue of a resolute-looking, bonnet-wearing pioneer woman cradling a baby in one arm and toting a bucket with the other was dedicated outside the National Frontier Trails Museum. There she stood until June 2013 when thieves pulled her down and broke her into pieces for sale as scrap metal. The dealer they approached recognized what was left of the statue and turned them down. He also turned them in. Two men and a woman were arrested, tried, and convicted for the felony theft. Remnants of the statue, however, were never located. Sculptor Charles Goslin of Shawnee created a new statue. That $40,000 work went up in 2017. In this incarnation, she has lost her bucket and now holds her infant with both arms.

Like Fathers, Like Sons

James "Jim Crow" Chiles rode with William Quantrill's guerillas. Most Civil War veterans lived law-abiding lives, but not Chiles. He was said to have killed at least nine men—not counting those killed during the war. But a Saturday night drunk that extended into Sunday proved to be his final spree. That day, September 21, 1873, as Deputy Marshal **James Peacock** (1824–1914) walked toward his office on the west side of the town square, his twenty-three-year-old son Charles (1850–1933) told him that Chiles had slapped him. Reacting as much as father as a lawman, Peacock said loudly that if Chiles wanted a fight, he could have it. Confident someone in town would report that to

Chiles, Peacock went to his upstairs office and strapped on the six-shooter he seldom wore. Walking back downstairs, he saw Chiles coming out of a nearby hotel. He had gotten the word. Approaching Peacock, Chiles slapped him just like he had his son. As the two men began fighting, Chiles's pistol fell from his pocket. His twelve-year-old son Elijah (1860–1873) picked it up and shot the officer in the back. In self-defense, the wounded Peacock fired and hit the elder Chiles in the head. Charles Peacock pulled his own handgun and shot Chiles's son, who died five days later. Deputy Peacock recovered and went on to have a career as a respected judge. He carried the bullet near his spine for the rest of his long life. No one appreciated the significance at the time, but Chiles's widow was the sister of Martha Ellen Young Truman, mother of future President Harry Truman.

The unusual gunfight between two father-son combatants took place on Liberty Street, just west of the town square. James J. "Jim Crow" Chiles is buried in **Woodlawn Cemetery** (701 South Noland Rd.; division 1, section 4, block 26, lot 5, space 9) along with his son Elijah "Little Lige" Chiles (division 1, section 5, block 1, lot 5, space 1). Judge Peacock also lies in Woodlawn Cemetery (division 1, section 4, block 8, lot 5, space 9). For all his accomplishments, Peacock has only a simple, flat tombstone bearing his name and dates of birth and death. His son, gunfight participant Charles Peacock, is buried in the **Old Bolles Cemetery** (GPS coordinates: N37° 43.76', W92° 43.45') in Lebanon, Missouri.

1859 Jail and Marshal's Home

Across the Old West, most town and county jails looked like jails: Sturdy stone or brick buildings with bars on the windows and steel cells inside. Some had an intimidating castle-like look, but there was no mistaking the structure's purpose. By contrast, the lockup in Independence, and those in a few other Missouri towns, were different. In 1859, a two-story, Federal-style, red-brick building went up on the town square. Now the **1859 Jail,**

Marshal's Home, and Museum (217 North Main St.; 816-252-1892), the building looked more like an inn or residence than what it really was, which was where the town marshal lived and had his office. The back half of the building, constructed of limestone blocks, housed the hoosegow. Guerilla fighter William Quantrill spent some time in the jail, and later, outlaw Frank James spent six months in one of the cells. The old jail continued in use until 1933 and in the mid-1950s stood in danger of being torn down when the Kansas City Historical Society acquired and restored it for use as a museum.

Frank James's Grave

Jesse James's old brother Frank survived his outlaw days and tried a variety of ways to support himself before he and Cole Younger teamed up one more time; this time not as outlaws, but co-owners of "The Great Cole Younger and Frank James Historical Wild West," a traveling show. The effort flopped, however, and old age caught up with Frank on February 18, 1915, when he died in the by-then historic family home. The grave is in **Hill Park Cemetery** (20th Street and Maywood Avenue), next to his wife's final resting place. One ground-level stone marks their graves, which are enclosed by a low stone wall.

JEFFERSON CITY (COLE COUNTY)

Jefferson City has been Missouri's capital since 1826, but whether the town would remain the seat of government was iffy until Governor John Miller pushed for construction of a substantial stone prison there, a project begun in 1834. The old prison still stands, along with forty-six other sites on the National Register of Historic Places.

The Walls

Inmates called the castle-like original structure and its later additions "The Walls." Law enforcement called it the **Missouri State Penitentiary** (115 Lafayette St.; 866-998-6998). Completed in 1836, the prison was expanded over the years as Missouri grew, and remained in use until 2004. By then, it was the oldest continually operating prison west of the Mississippi. The state retained ownership of the historic facility and reopened it as a museum. Thanks to numerous executions, prison riots, escapes, and murders of convicts and prison guards, *Time Magazine* dubbed the prison "the bloodiest 47 acres in America." Wild West–era outlaws who did time in the prison include members of the Reno gang and Bill Ryan, an alum of the James-Younger gang. The 1888 former warden's residence, known as the **Colonel Darwin Marmaduke House,** has been converted into a museum with prison artifacts and replica of a typical cell. The **Jefferson City Convention and Visitors Bureau** (700 East Capitol Ave.; 573-632-2820) offers tours.

Jefferson began as a steamboat landing on the Missouri River, and river traffic was integral to the town's economy until the arrival of the railroad. The **Jefferson Landing State Historic Site** (100 Jefferson St.; 573-751-2854) opened in 1976. The center piece of the site is an 1839 stone structure known as the Lohman Building. Over the years it accommodated a store, warehouse, tavern, hotel, and telegraph office. Part of the building, which came to be known as "the landing," housed a hotel popular with rivermen and lawmakers.

The **Missouri State Museum** (201 West Capitol Ave.; 573-751-3339) occupies the 1917 statehouse's ground floor. On the third floor, in the House of Representatives' lounge, the walls are covered with a series of murals painted by Thomas Hart Benton in 1935. Called *A Social History of the State of Missouri*, the artwork depicts the state's development through events in the lives of everyday people, from fur trapping to the cattle industry to politics. One of the images is of Frank and Jesse James robbing a bank. State capitols generally display portraits of former governors and lawmakers, a few known to have been corrupt, but Missouri's capitol is the only one commemorating two gun-toting outlaws.

KANSAS CITY (JACKSON COUNTY)

French fur traders opened a trading post where the Kansas River meets the Missouri in 1821, but permanent Euro-American settlement did not begin until the early 1830s when Reverend Isaac McCoy and his family moved to the area. In 1833, McCoy's son John built a two-story log building as a combination mercantile business and residence. Two years later he laid out a town he called Westport. In 1839, McCoy and other investors filed a plat for another prospective community, the town of Kansas. When the future state of Kansas became a territory, the Missouri town was renamed Kansas City to avoid confusion. After the Civil War, Kansas City eclipsed Westport in size and significance after gaining its first rail connection in 1866. Four years later, Kansas City opened a stockyard that made it a major western cattle market. By the 1890s, having annexed Westport, Kansas City had become a major city second only to St. Louis.

As with other large cities in the West, Kansas City offers history-minded visitors a wide range of interesting sites, from Union Station, site of the 1933 Kansas City Massacre (though not part of Wild West history it may as well have been), to the National WWI Museum and Memorial opened in 2006. For more insight into historical attractions not covered here, check with the **Kansas City Visitors Center** (1321 Baltimore Ave.; 816-691-3800). The Westport Historical Society has its offices and a museum in the 1855 **Harris-Kearny House** (4000 Baltimore Ave.; 816-561-1821).

Old West Time Capsule

The steamboat *Arabia*, carrying 130 passengers and two hundred tons of cargo, sank in the Missouri River just north of Kansas City on September 5, 1856. The passengers safely made it to shore, but all the supplies on board—merchandise and food that had been on its way to the western frontier—went down with the vessel. In time, the river changed course, leaving the hulk of the steamboat buried under several feet of sediment. In 1988 a privately funded archeological investigation located the wreck and excavated it. The archeologists discovered that sediment had left the steamboat's contents nearly perfectly preserved, a massive time capsule of everyday goods that helped settle the West, from beaver hats and canned pickles to rifles and whiskey.

The **Arabia Steamboat Museum** (400 Grand Blvd.; 816-471-1856) is owned and operated by the families who discovered the wreck and continue to excavate it. Opened in 1991 in the city's historic River Market area, the museum displays thousands of items recovered from the riverboat along with portions of the vessel. The boat's original engine and larboard support structure are featured, along with a twenty-eight-foot reproduction of its paddle wheel.

Bent-Ward House

The story of the **Bent-Ward House** (1032 West 55th St.) is the story of the Old and New West in microcosm. In the 1830s Mormons purchased the land that included the future homesite with plans to convert the American Indians in the area, but that didn't work out. The land ended up in the hands of Brigham Young's lawyer, Alexander Doniphan. Doniphan sold it to a farmer who worked the land for a time before selling it in 1858 to frontiersman William Bent. Bent built a two-story brick house on the property and continued farming operations. During the Civil War, the Battle of Westport was fought in Bent's cornfields, though he was not there at the time. When Bent died in Colorado in 1869, his American Indian wife conveyed the Missouri property in 1871 to Seth Ward, a former fur trapper, buffalo hunter, and trader who profited nicely as post sutler at Fort Laramie, Wyoming. After acquiring the property, Ward built a larger, more imposing brick house that incorporated the old Bent house. He went on to become a banker and real estate developer before his death in 1903. The house stayed in the Ward family until 1942. After that, it saw a variety of owners. Still privately owned, it has been renovated and is periodically opened to the public for Kansas City Symphony fundraising events. Two historical markers on the grounds offer a condensed history of the house.

Alexander Majors House

The Pony Express didn't last long, made obsolete by the telegraph and a casualty of the Civil War, but the house built by Pony Express owner Alexander Majors still stands. Majors was a partner in the freighting company of Russell, Majors and Waddell, a significant influencer on the growth of Kansas City and the development of the West. Built facing west only feet away from the Kansas-Missouri border in 1856, the restored home is listed on the National Register of Historic Places. But it almost didn't make it. By the 1920s, it stood in ruins and was in danger of being razed. In 1930, Louisa Johnston, Majors's great-granddaughter, bought the house, restored it, and lived in it until her death in 1979. The further refurbished two-story frame antebellum house (8201 State Line Rd.; 816-444-1858) was opened to the public in 1984. Guided or self-guided tours are available.

A nine-and-a-half-foot bronze statue in **Pioneer Park** (Broadway Boulevard and Westport Road; 816-513-7500), commemorates three key figures in the history of Westport and Kansas City: Pony Express founder Alexander Majors, Westport and Kansas City co-founder John Calvin McCoy, and famed mountain man Jim Bridger (1804–1881). The piece was commissioned by the Westport Historical Society and Native Sons of Kansas City and dedicated in 1987.

Bridger spent the last fifteen years of his life in Westport. He farmed a large tract in the vicinity of present 103rd Street and State Line and in 1866 began operating a store at 504 Westport Road. The two-story brick structure, one of the oldest buildings in Westport, still stands and accommodates a restaurant-bar. Following his death at age seventy-seven, Bridger was buried in an unmarked grave in a small private cemetery not far from his residence. In 1904, his remains were exhumed and buried in **Mount Washington Cemetery** (614 South Brookside Ave.) in Independence.

KEARNEY (CLAY COUNTY)

Kearney was the outlaw Jesse James's hometown, but he wasn't born there. That's because the town did not yet exist when he came into the world in 1847. The town dates from 1867, when John Lawrence purchased land and platted a townsite in anticipation of the approaching Hannibal and St. Joseph Railroad. At one point, as many as sixty trains passed through the community, bringing people and prosperity, but in the modern era one of the town's driving economic forces has been its famous homeboy.

In 1845 the Reverend Robert James and his young wife, Zerelda, moved into a log farmhouse a couple miles north of future Kearney in Clay County. They already had one son, Frank, and on September 5, 1847, Zerelda gave birth to a second boy, Jesse Woodson James. But much more happened in that house than that. When the Civil War began, the family sided with the South and in 1863 Frank James joined the Confederate guerillas. A year later, Union soldiers came to the Jameses' farm looking for Frank. By this time Zerelda had remarried after Robert James died in the California gold fields in 1850. The soldiers tortured Jesse's stepfather, Dr. Reuben Samuel, and beat the teenaged Jesse. The incident only solidified the James boys' hatred of Yankees, a key motivation in the path they took after the war.

Years later, on the night of January 26, 1875, a party of armed men, likely led by a Pinkerton Detective Agency operative, surrounded the Jameses' house looking for Frank and Jesse, who by that time were nationally known and highly sought after outlaws. They were not there, but the men did not know that. Expecting to flush the two young men out of the house, someone tossed several flares through a window. One of them unexpectedly exploded, killing James's half-brother Archie and tearing off Zerelda's right arm.

That was the last violence the family farm would see, but in 1882 Jesse's career ended when Robert Ford shot him in the back (see St. Joseph, Missouri). Fearful that someone might steal her son's body and put it on exhibition, Zeralda had Jesse buried in front of her house. But she wasn't above profiting from Jesse's notoriety. She soon began giving tours of the house and for twenty-five cents she would let visitors keep a rock from near the grave. Following his mother's death in 1911, Frank moved into the old house and began offering tours for a half-dollar a head. When Frank died there in 1915, his son Robert took up what had become the family business—making money off their long dead but increasingly famous relative. Other James descendants kept the house open to the public until Clay County bought it and forty-nine surrounding acres in 1978. A year later, the site reopened to the public. **The James Farm** museum (21216 James Farm Rd.; 816-736-8500) maintains the nation's largest collection of James family relics and other material, including a pair of Jesse James's boots.

Jesse James's Grave

When James's remains were exhumed from the front yard of his birthplace in 1902, he was reburied in **Mount Olivet Cemetery** (GPS coordinates: N39° 22.05', W94° 21.88') in Kearney. The outlaw's widow, his mother, his stepfather, and his half-brother are also buried there in the Samuel-James family plot. The cemetery, established in 1868, is on the south side of East 6th Street just past the railroad tracks.

The **Kearney Historic Museum** (101 South Jefferson St.; 816-903-1856) focuses on the history of James's hometown, but there's also an exhibit on the outlaw and his family. The most singular artifact displayed is a large, rounded safe with a square base on rollers once used by the Kearney Trust Bank. But what makes it interesting has nothing to do with the money it once held. After Frank James died in 1915, his body was cremated. From then until 1944, the urn containing his ashes was kept in this safe. When his widow died that year, James's ashes were buried next to her ashes.

LAMAR (BARTON COUNTY)

Laid out in 1856, Lamar was named for a Georgia poet who became the first vice president of the Republic of Texas, Mirabeau B. Lamar. Not far from the Kansas border, the southwest Missouri county seat for a time was home to one of the Wild West's most iconic figures, Wyatt Earp.

The Constable and Aurilla

On November 17, 1869, county officials appointed a young man named Wyatt Earp as town constable to replace the man who had just resigned the office—his father. Early the following year, on January 10, 1870, the twenty-one-year-old lawman married Aurilla (while Aurilla is generally accepted as the spelling of her first name, she is often referred to in print as Urilla Sutherland), the beginning of a short husband-wife relationship and a long-enduring mystery. In November that year, his appointment about the expire, Earp won election to a full term by a vote of 157 to 108. While he surely found the voting results satisfying, only a short time later, tragedy struck with the death of his new wife. Though grieving Aurilla's sudden passing, Earp played fast and loose with the fines and fees he collected in his official capacity. When county officials discovered that the young officer had taken in more than $200 that should have gone into the county treasury, he slipped out of town.

The mystery he left behind is symbolized by a crude concrete grave marker in Lamar that reads only "Wife of Wyatt." While it is known that some of his relatives placed the homemade monument in the 1940s, the mystery is whether it truly marks Aurilla's grave or whether her remains lie in Milford, Missouri; Pineville, Missouri; Palatine, Illinois; or even Cherokee County, Kansas. Another aspect of the mystery is whether Wyatt's bride died of typhoid or following the birth of a stillborn child. The "Wife of Wyatt" marker stands in **East Cemetery** (16th and Hagny Streets).

While Wyatt departed Lamar for good, soon followed by his parents, he left some relatives behind. Earp's first cousin, Walter Earp, lived from 1920 to 1945 in the small frame house where future President Harry S. Truman had been born in 1884. Walter Earp's son Everette lived there until his death in 1956. The **Truman House** (1009 Truman St.; 417-682-2279) was then purchased and deeded to the State of Missouri as a historic site.

The Barton County Chamber of Commerce is coordinating an effort to develop a park named for Earp at the intersection of 10th and Broadway Streets on the northeast corner of the courthouse square. **Wyatt Earp Park** will feature a statue of the town's legendary one-time marshal standing next to his wife, murals telling the young couple's story, benches, landscaping, and a covered pavilion for musical and other outdoor events.

In honor of their hometown legend, Lamar celebrates its **Wyatt Earp Fallfest** each October.

LEE'S SUMMIT (JACKSON COUNTY)

Founded as Strother in the mid-1840s by William B. Howard, who named the settlement after his wife Maria D. Strother, the community got its current—if confusing—name in 1865.

Townsfolk had decided to honor an early settler named Pleasant John Graves Lea, who had been killed by Kansas Jayhawkers in 1862. His land holdings included the highest point in the area, hence the addition of "Summit" to the name. But when the Missouri Pacific Railroad came through, the name was misspelled as "Lees Summit" with no apostrophe. The possessive was later added, but the misspelling stuck. Another version has the town named for Confederal general Robert E. Lee, but the Lea-to-Lee's story is accepted history. Regardless of who the town was named for, one of its native sons became one of the Wild West's most notorious—and interesting—outlaws.

Born at Lee's Summit, **Thomas Coleman Younger** (1844–1916) spent twenty-five years in prison after pleading guilty to murder in Jesse and Frank James's bloody Northfield raid in 1876 (see Northfield, Minnesota). Paroled from the Minnesota state prison in 1901, Younger received a full pardon two years later. He worked for a time as a tombstone salesman and insurance agent before partnering with Frank James in a Wild West show venture. He went on to travel extensively, lecturing on the evils of crime. He died at age seventy-two in his hometown on March 21, 1916, and is buried in **Lee's Summit Cemetery** (806 Southeast 3rd St.; lot 12). Also buried there are his outlaw brothers Robert (1853–1889), who died in prison, and Jim (1848–1902), who was paroled along with Cole but committed suicide in a St. Paul, Minnesota, hotel room because the terms of his parole prevented him from marrying the newspaper reporter with whom he'd fallen in love, Alix Muller. The boys' mother, Bursheba L. (Fristoe) Younger (1816–1870) is also buried there.

LIBERTY (CLAY COUNTY)

A cannon's distant boom once meant prosperity for the Missouri River town of Liberty. In the community's early days, any time a passenger or cargo-laden steamboat approached, the vessel's captain customarily ordered the firing of a small cannon to signal his pending arrival. Incorporated in 1829, Liberty claims to be the second oldest town west of the Mississippi. Following the Civil War, the westward expansion of the nation's railroad system ended most of Liberty's river commerce, but the town continued as a bustling trade center.

Liberty has five historic districts with numerous historical structures. **Historic Downtown Liberty, Inc.** has a visitor center (117 North Main St.; 816-781-3575) that offers a series of self-guided tours, with audio, including one featuring Jesse James–related sites and another of sites connected to Alexander Doniphan.

Opened in a restored antebellum building in 1965, the **Clay County Museum and Historical Society** (14 North Main; 816-792-1849) has three floors of exhibits relating the county's history.

He Helped Change the Map of the West

In 1833, Alexander William Doniphan, a young lawyer originally from Kentucky, moved to Liberty and began a legal practice. He also joined a state militia company, the Liberty Blues. That was the beginning of a military career that would play a major role in changing the map of the American West.

Having quickly risen in rank, in 1838 Doniphan led a contingent of state troops against Mormons under Joseph Smith. Following the religious leader's arrest, Doniphan refused a direct order to execute him, asserting it was illegal. Instead, Smith and several of his followers were put on trial. Doniphan, though he did not personally follow their belief, participated in their defense.

When the Mexican War began in 1848, hundreds of Missouri men enlisted to join the fight, including Doniphan. On the muster rolls as a private, he was elected as colonel of the First Regiment of Missouri Mounted Volunteers, part of Gen. Stephen Kearny's Army of the West. Soon the thirty-nine-year-old colonel led his command on an epic march from Fort Leavenworth in Kansas Territory to Santa Fe. There he took control of New Mexico and developed a legal code later used in organizing New Mexico's territorial government. From Santa Fe the regiment, some one thousand men strong, moved south across the desert to Mexico, prevailing in a brief engagement with Mexican troops north of present El Paso.

From the Rio Grande, Doniphan proceeded to Chihuahua City, where in the February 1847 Battle of the Sacramento River he defeated a force of five thousand with few casualties. From the captured city, Doniphan moved across northern Mexico to join forces with Gen. Zachary Taylor. Their enlistments about to expire and the war won, Doniphan marched to Point Isabel, Texas. From there he and his command traveled by ship across the Gulf of Mexico to New Orleans where he received a hero's welcome. The Missouri lawyer-soldier had marched more than 3,500 miles, a campaign still considered the second-longest in military history.

While Doniphan was an enslaver, he favored a phase-out of the institution and argued vehemently against secession. When the Civil War began, he refused a general's commission in the Union army and moved to St. Louis for the duration of the conflict. After the war, he and his wife settled in Richmond, Missouri, where he died in 1887. He is buried in Liberty's **Fairview Cemetery** (Terrace Avenue and West Shrader Street; block 95, lot 15, space 2).

The Big Robbery

Clay County Savings Association cashier Greenup Bird and his young clerk (and son) William were sitting at their respective desks when two men wearing blue army overcoats walked in the bank. It was a cold, snowy day, and both men paused at the stove in the small lobby to warm their hands. Then one of them approached the counter and asked for change for a ten-dollar bill. When William stood to accommodate the customer, he saw a revolver pointed at him. That man, quickly followed by the second, jumped over the counter, handed the clerk a sack, and told him to fill it with all the money in the walk-in safe. While William loaded the sack with gold and silver coins, the second gunman told the cashier to round up all the cash as well. When Bird moved too slowly for the impatient robber, he was hit in the back of his head with a six-shooter. After collecting nearly $60,000—hundreds of thousands in today's dollars—the men ordered father and son into the vault and closed the heavy door behind them.

Bird waited until he thought the men had gone, found the door had not been locked, and rushed to the window in time to see a dozen or more horsemen galloping down the street firing pistols as they headed out of town. One of the rounds struck and killed a nineteen-year-old college student. As soon as townspeople understood what had happened, two groups of armed citizens rode out in pursuit of the raiders. They tracked them to the Missouri River, just across from Sibley, but never caught up to the robbers.

Though it is irrefutable that two men robbed the Liberty bank on February 13, 1866, while their associates waited outside, no one was ever arrested for the crime. No compelling evidence links Frank and Jesse James to the crime, but historians say the pair may have been among the raiders that day. What history buffs *can* take to the bank is the fact that no matter who pulled the holdup, it was the first daylight robbery of a financial institution in US history.

Since it would not be until the twentieth century that the federal government insured bank deposits, the Clay County Savings Association went belly up soon after the robbery. Over the years, the building served as home to two other financial institutions and other commercial enterprises before its interior was restored to its original appearance and opened as the **Jesse James Bank Museum** (103 North Water St.; 816-736-8510). Built in 1859, the two-story, Federal-style brick building still has its original vault.

MANSFIELD (WRIGHT COUNTY)

This small town in the Ozarks was platted in 1882 by F.M. Mansfield and the community was named for him. But it turned out to be someone else's last name that would transform the community into a heritage tourism destination.

In the summer of 1894, Almanzo Wilder, his wife Laura Ingalls Wilder, and their daughter Rose traveled in a two-seated hack from South Dakota to Mansfield. They had heard that apples grew particularly well in this part of Missouri and bought forty acres just outside of town. They called it the Rocky Ridge Farm.

At first they lived in a log cabin, but over the next seventeen years, room by room they built a two-story house finally completed in 1913. They did quite well as farmers until the American economy collapsed during the Great Depression. Laura had been doing some newspaper and magazine writing for nearly twenty years, but the onset of harsh economic times is what convinced her to take up another form of commodity production—writing novels. Her *Little House on the Prairie* series, inspired by her family's experiences on the Western plains, proved highly popular and she became a best-selling author.

Wilder remained in Mansfield until her death in 1957. The family farmhouse, a National Historic Landmark, houses the **Laura Ingalls Wilder Historic Home and Museum** (3060 Highway A; 877-924-

7126), which has the nation's largest collection of Wilder material. Also open to visitors is a rock house purchased for her parents by daughter Rose. Wilder did some of her writing there, though most of her work was completed in the larger farmhouse.

MEXICO (AUDRAIN COUNTY)

Improbable as it may seem, ten places in the US are named Mexico, but only one Mexico lies west of the Mississippi—Mexico, Missouri. The town began as New Mexico, but during the Mexican War, the "New" got dropped.

A Lesson Learned Too Late

Since it got broken in half, all the words on Jim Berry's marble tombstone are no longer legible, but the inscription once read: "James F. Berry Killed by H. Glascock." But there's more to it than that. **James Fulkerson Berry**, born to a Callaway County farming family in 1838, later joined the Sam Bass gang when the outlaw operated in the Black Hills of then Dakota Territory. On September 18, 1877, with Bass and four others, he was involved in the robbery of a Union Pacific train near Big Springs, Nebraska. The holdup netted the bandits $60,000 in gold.

Berry departed for home with his share of the loot, enough money to have lasted the rest of his life. Unfortunately for him, the rest of his life would only be a few weeks. Instead of spending the $20 gold pieces discretely, a few at a time, he went to each of Mexico's three banks and exchanged $9,000 worth of the stolen gold for that amount in cash. The banks apparently did not question it, but when the coins reached the federal depository in St. Louis, that institution correctly deduced that it had come from the Big Springs robbery.

County sheriff Henry Glascock soon held a warrant for Berry's arrest, which led to the young man's second mistake. When confronted by the lawman, instead of surrendering, Berry took flight. Only intending to stop him from running, the sheriff aimed low and peppered him in the legs with a load of birdshot. Though painful, the small wounds probably would not have been fatal if infection had not set in. Two days later, on October 21, 1877, Berry died.

Berry, his mother, and other family members are buried in **Liberty Cemetery** (also known as Liberty Christian Church Cemetery) two miles north of the Callaway County town of Shamrock at the southwest corner of CR-1044 and CR-1063. The two halves of Berry's tombstone, set flat in a concrete square, are in lot 42, tier 16.

In Mexico, twenty-three miles from Shamrock, the **Audrain County Historical Society** (504 Muldrow St.; 573-581-3910) operates three museums focusing on various aspects of the county's history.

NEW MADRID (NEW MADRID COUNTY)

Land speculator and Indian trader George Morgan, a Revolutionary War veteran, founded New Madrid on high ground overlooking the Mississippi River in 1789. Spain then held much of North America and that's why Morgan named his town after the old Spanish city.

At first New Madrid amounted to little more than a trading post, but by 1811 it had grown to a community of some four hundred people. With the area now owned by the expansion-minded US government, keelboats and flat-bottomed boats carrying people and goods along the river drove the economy and business improved even more with the coming of the newly invented steamboat.

In the dead of night on December 16, 1811, a huge earthquake struck. Its epicenter was actually where the present town of Marked Tree, Arkansas, now stands, but New Madrid was the only populated area at the time, so the cataclysmic geological event became known as the **New Madrid Earthquake**. The most powerful earthquake in North American history, it was actually a series of strong seismic events that continued into the following year.

William Pierce happened to be on a flat-bottomed boat just downriver from New Madrid when the first of five major earthquakes struck. He described the event in a letter to a New York newspaper:

Everywhere Nature itself seem tottering on the verge of disso-lution. . . . The earth, river, etc., torn with furious convulsions, opened in huge trenches. There through a thousand vents sulphu-rous streams gushed from its very bowels leaving vast and almost unfathomable caverns. The bed of the river, was excessively agi-tated, whilst the water assumed a turbid and boiling appearance. Never was a scene more replete with terrific threatenings of death.

Indeed, the upheaval for a time even reversed the flow of the river. No one knows how many people it killed, but the number surely surpasses a hundred. The earthquakes altered the landscape of the Mississippi valley. On the bright side, since many thought the event presaged the end of the world, church attendance spiked for a time.

In a former riverfront saloon, the **New Madrid Historical Museum** (1 Main St.; 543-748-5944) tells the story of the earth-quake and covers the town's post-earthquake history.

OTTERVILLE (COOPER COUNTY)

Platted in 1837 and first known as Elkton, by the time a post office had been established here in 1848 the community had been renamed Otterville for nearby Otter Creek.

Alleged Jesse James gang robbery sites are almost as common as "George Washington slept here" locations in the northeastern states, but there's no doubt that the train robbery that took place near here on the night of July 7, 1876, was the work of the brothers James and Younger and their colleagues in crime. Stopping a Missouri Pacific passenger train by piling railroad ties on the track, the bandits escaped with more than $18,000. Numerous warning shots had been fired, but no one was hurt during the holdup.

A gray granite historical marker summarizing the crime stands just east of Otterville in **Brownfield Roadside Park** (GPS coordinates: N38° 42.34', W92° 57.94') on Old US 50. From the park, visitors can look downhill at the man-made cut where the robbery took place. Initially known as Rock Cut, the narrow point along the railroad right-of-way has been known as Robber's Cut since the robbery. The Missouri Pacific Railroad has since been absorbed by the Union Pacific Railroad. Union Pacific freight trains and Amtrak passenger trains still pass through the cut.

PRINCETON (MERCER COUNTY)

Just south of the Iowa border, Princeton was settled in the spring of 1846. The town was named for the Revolutionary War Battle of Princeton, and the county named for Continental army Brig. Gen. Hugh Mercer, who died in the fight.

A decade after the founding of the town, on May 1, 1856, Robert W. Canary and his sixteen-year-old wife Charlotte became the parents of a daughter. Their first child, they named her Martha Jane. The family remained in Mercer County until 1864 when the girl's father decided to go west to the gold fields in Montana. Two years later, Charlotte—by then having given birth to five more children—died. Her husband left Montana for Salt Lake City, Utah, where he died in 1867. Martha Jane and her siblings were on their own. The rest of her life could not be called particularly successful, but she became one of the best-known women of the West—**Calamity Jane**.

A stone historical marker on the town square (Broadway and Main Streets) notes that Calamity Jane was born just east of town and "became a symbol of the wild west." Four miles north of town off US 65 is the **Calamity Jane Roadside Park**, where a state historical marker gives a history of Mercer County and mentions that Calamity Jane was born near Princeton. Capitalizing on one of its principal claims to fame, every September, the town puts on a festival called Calamity Jane Days. The highlight of the annual event is the selection of a young lady as Miss Calamity Jane.

Richmond (Ray County)

Named for Richmond, Virginia, decades before that Southern city became the capital of the Confederacy, this northwestern Missouri community was founded in 1828. With a life-size bronze statue, the town remembers as a principled hero a man whose military acumen helped the US gain possession of the Southwest, while also accepting that it is the burial place of another Wild West figure who went down in infamy as a cowardly killer.

Moving to Richmond at age fifty-two, still mourning the recent death of his wife, Alexander Doniphan (see Liberty, Missouri) spent the final fourteen years of his life practicing law here. He also established the Ray County Savings Bank and served as its president. Following his death on August 8, 1887, his body was sent to Liberty for burial, but the residents of Richmond did not forget him. On July 29, 1918, more than twenty thousand people gathered on the lawn of the Ray County Courthouse for the dedication of a larger-than-life statue of Doniphan sculpted by Missouri artist Frederick C. Hibbard.

Here Lies "The Dirty Little Coward . . ."

When Jesse James's killer Robert Ford (1862–1892) was killed by Edward O'Kelley in Creede, Colorado, he was buried there. Later, his family had his remains exhumed and shipped to Missouri for reburial in his hometown of Richmond. Ford is buried in **Richmond Cemetery** (far west end of Main Street, adjacent to Sunny Slope Cemetery). A sign near the cemetery entrance points to the burial site. Also buried here is Ford's brother Charles (1857–1884), who conspired with him to kill James. Originally sentenced to hang for his role in the murder, Charles was pardoned by the governor. But no pardon was forthcoming in the court of public opinion. Roundly disliked, and worried that someone might kill him, Charles preempted that by committing suicide on May 4, 1884.

The **Ray County Museum** (901 West Royle St.; 816-776-2305) focuses on the history and culture of the area.

ST. LOUIS (ST. LOUIS COUNTY)

St. Louis began in 1764 as a French trading post at the confluence of the Missouri and Mississippi Rivers. Following the 1803 Louisiana Purchase, it became the departure point for American western exploration. After the first riverboat tied up there in 1817, the city rapidly evolved as the young nation's western-most metropolis. When the 1874 bridging of the Mississippi made possible rail connections to the rest of the nation, St. Louis exploded in population. By the 1890s, with more than three hundred thousand residents, it had become the nation's fourth-largest city.

Given its long history, St. Louis is a veritable resort for history buffs, with several days' worth of historic sites and museums to see. **Gateway Arch National Park** is the place to start (see below), followed by the **Missouri Historical Museum** (5700 Lindell Blvd.; 314-746-4599). Operated by the Missouri Historical Society (created in 1866), the museum has exhibits and an extensive collection of archival material relating to the city and state's history.

Along with earlier forms of transportation, railroads helped build the West. The **National Museum of Transportation** (3015 Barrett School Rd., Kirkwood; 314-965-6212) has the world's largest collection of rolling stock. Founded in 1944, the museum has more than 190 major exhibits. Another railroad site is **Union Station** (1820 Market St.; 314-923-3900). Opened in 1894, it was listed on the National Register of Historic Places in 1970.

The Gateway Arch

The nation's tallest monument, the Gateway Arch, symbolizes St. Louis's heritage as the one-time gateway to the West. The stainless-steel structure, completed in 1965, rises 630 feet above the riverfront and is the center piece of ninety-one-acre **Gateway Arch National Park** (11 North 4th St.; 877-982-1410) known until 2018 as the Jefferson National Expansion Memorial.

With a focus on St. Louis's role in the saga, the **Museum at the Gateway Arch** interprets the two-century history of westward expansion from the founding of St. Louis to the building of its iconic arch. Opened in 2018 with interactive story galleries, the museum is a new, reimagined replacement for the park's original museum, the Museum of Westward Expansion. The new museum reflects the perspectives of all the cultures involved—even its terrazzo floor is an exhibit mapping the trails of North America that brought people to the western half of the continent.

The third major component of the park is the old **St. Louis County Courthouse** (11 North 4th St.; 314-655-1600) built of brick and stone and expanded through the early 1860s. St. Louis County had outgrown its original courthouse by the mid-1830s, and construction began on a second one in 1839. The Greek Revival–style building has a three-story dome (added in the early 1860s) modeled after Saint Peter's Basilica in Vatican City. The dome has four lunettes with paintings done in the 1880s depicting four pivotal events in St. Louis history to that point. Two landmark Supreme Court cases began here—the 1847 suit in which Dred Scott, an enslaved man, and his wife Harriet sued for their freedom (and won), and the 1872 suit brought by Virginia Minor, who had been arrested for voting in a St. Louis election. The high court upheld the notion of male-only voting, but the case helped bring about the women's suffrage movement.

St. Louis County vacated the old courthouse in 1930. A decade later, following complicated litigation over ownership of the land on which the building stood, the property was deeded to the federal government. The National Park Service took over the building in 1940, renovated it, and opened it as a museum in 1943.

Pauly Jail Building Company

A St. Louis–based company that produced an unusual product did what it could to make the West a little less wild.

Founded in 1856, the P. J. Pauly and Brother Company specialized in riverboat repair along St. Louis's busy riverfront. German immigrant Peter Joseph Pauly (1832–1917) and his younger brother John (1835–1899) were mechanics and blacksmiths who, at the height of the steamboat era, had no shortage of business. But railroads scuttled river traffic. That's when Peter had an idea. He and his brother could use their skills building something essential for civilizing the frontier—jails. At first, they manufactured individual cells anchored to flat wagons that could be moved from Wild West boomtown to boomtown. Their product sold well, and in 1885, they renamed their business, becoming the Pauly Jail Building and Manufacturing Company. Sales representatives traveled the West negotiating contracts with territorial, state, and local governments for the manufacture and installation of prefabricated jails. Meanwhile the company continued to innovate, developing hardened steel bars, the concept of large day rooms, and other improvements. The firm obtained various patents, including improved locking devices and their most unusual product, rotating jails.

Peter Joseph Pauly is buried in St. Louis's historic **Calvary Cemetery** (5239 West Florissant Ave.; section 017, lot 0516). His brother John's grave is in the same cemetery (section 017, lot 0515).

The jail manufacturing plant stood at 2215 DeKalb Street but has since been razed. The company headquarters is now in Noblesville, Indiana, but Pauly still has a satellite office in St. Louis. There is no corporate museum, but the company's website (paulyjail.com/legacy) has more background on this historic if little-known firm.

ST. GENEVIEVE (ST. GENEVIEVE COUNTY)

St. Genevieve grew from a French settlement on the west bank of the Missouri founded in the late 1740s. A devastating flood forced its removal about two miles to its current site in 1790. It has remained a small town, most of its many historic structures still intact.

Despite the town's old-world heritage, something decidedly Western happened here on May 27, 1873, when four men held up the St. Genevieve Savings Association. The robbers never faced charges here, but St. Louis police later attributed the job to the Jesse James and Cole Younger gang.

Its narrow streets and prevailing French colonial–style architecture gives this old river town a distinctive European feel. But there are also residences built by German immigrants and nineteenth-century Victorian structures. With more than eight hundred historic structures, the town was designated a National Historic Landmark in 1959. The **St. Genevieve Museum** (3rd and Merchant Streets; 573-883-3466), in addition to its interpretive exhibits, offers self-guided tours of the town.

ST. JOSEPH (BUCHANAN COUNTY)

From his trading post on a bend of the Missouri River where St. Joseph would later rise, Joseph Robidoux built a profitable fur business in the 1820s extending all the way to the Rocky Mountains. In 1843 he turned down speculators who wanted to buy his land along the river, had a townsite platted, and began selling lots for what would become St. Joseph. With the discovery of gold in California in 1848, the river port became an important departure point for westward expansion.

The best place to start your visit is the **St. Joseph Visitors Bureau** (North Woodbine Road; 816-232-1839).

Pony Express Headquarters

In 1858 John Patee built a luxury four-story, 140-room hotel epitomizing what cities like St. Joseph and Independence were all about at the time—the last vestige of civilization for westward-bound travelers. And so was the new hostelry. Patee's hotel featured hot and cold running water and a natural "air conditioning" system facilitated by a cupola. Beyond the Missouri River, soft beds, hot baths, and easy eating were hard to come by.

Two years later, on April 3, 1860, the hotel became the headquarters for the Pony Express. Founders William Russell, Alexander Majors, and William Waddell leased the first floor for their new enterprise, an effort to move mail by horseback from St. Joseph to Sacramento in only ten days. The **Pony Express** lasted eighteen months, and the **Patee Hotel** didn't fare much better. Patee tried to sell the property in a nationwide lottery in late 1864, but that proved unsuccessful.

After Patee finally did unload the hotel, it saw use as a college for women and again as a hotel under two different owners, the last time renamed the **World's Hotel**. When it closed in late 1882, the building stood vacant until it was converted into a garment factory in 1888. That enterprise remained in operation until the 1950s. The old hotel is now restored and operates as a museum by the Pony Express Historical Association (1202 Penn St.).

Until it shut down on Christmas Eve 1959, the **Buffalo Saloon** billed itself as the oldest whiskey emporium west of the Mississippi. Originally located at 4th and Edmond Streets, it was built in 1854. While the entire building no longer exists, in 1966 the Pony Express Historical Association purchased its ornate front and back bars and recreated the Wild West watering hole inside the **Patee House Museum**.

Pony Express Museum

An old stable that now houses a museum is where the Pony Express began on April 3, 1860, when rider William (Billie) Richardson rode from there to the Patee House Hotel to pick up the mochila—a type of leather saddlebag containing four lockable pockets to hold letters—and begin his historic ride westward. First known as Pike's Peak Stables, the roughly fifty-eight- by fifty-five-foot, one-story building was constructed of wood in 1858 to accommodate the horses owned by a local stagecoach and freight company. Two years later the stable was purchased for the new Pony Express and served as the transportation system's eastern terminus until the company went out of business in October 1861. In 1888 the structure was rebuilt with brick, possibly retaining some of the original interior frame. The old building was restored in 1950 and began its new life as the **Pony Express National Museum** (914 Penn St.; 816-232-8206). In 1970 it was added to the National Register of Historic Places and today features a series of large dioramas, artifacts, and maps interpreting the history of the short-lived but important communication system.

Tom Howard Dusts a Wall Hanging

During the Christmas season in 1881, Jesse James—who since moving his family to St. Joseph the month before had been posing as one Thomas Howard—rented a house on a high hill overlooking the **World's Hotel**.

The following spring, fugitive and cohorts Charley and Robert Ford (who had been staying in James's house) began planning a bank robbery that James thought "would be published all over the United States." Unknown to James, the two brothers were doing some planning of their own. What they had in mind, they believed, would net them even bigger money than their share of the proceeds from the holdup—the $10,000 reward being offered for James's arrest and conviction. The proclamation issued by Missouri Governor Thomas T. Crittenden was widely interpreted as meaning the outlaw was wanted "dead or alive." Given James's reputation, the Fords correctly calculated it would be far safer to collect on the outlaw's corpse than to try bringing him in alive.

On April 3, 1882, with James's family at home in another room, Robert Ford put a .44-caliber bullet behind James's right ear. The outlaw had risen to dust a picture on the mantel and Ford shot him from behind. The thirty-four-year-old legend was dead before he hit the floor.

The brothers Ford had made a bad calculation. They were arrested and charged with murder and while they were not convicted, they did not get the reward. Despite James's repute, few admired anyone who would shoot another man in the back.

James had been born in Missouri, died in Missouri, and of twenty-six major crimes he is believed to have committed, he pulled off eleven of them in his home state.

Now a museum, the home where James was killed originally stood at 1318 Lafayette Street. In 1939 the historic structure was turned into a tourist attraction. People gawked at a bullet hole in the wall that reputedly came from the death shot, but if it really was a bullet hole, it did not date from the time of the killing.

Robert Keatley and his wife bought the white frame house in 1977 and moved it to the grounds of the Patee House. Among the **James Museum**'s artifacts are items recovered from James's grave in 1995 (see Kearney, Missouri), including coffin handles, a small tie pin James wore the day he was killed, a Civil War bullet removed from his right lung area, and a casting of his skull that shows the fatal bullet hole behind his right ear. A lock of James's hair also is on display.

The **Buchanan County Courthouse** (411 Jules St.; 816-232-8206), built in 1873, saw the joint murder trial of the Ford brothers in 1882. Both were convicted of murder, but Governor Crittenden quickly pardoned them. The brothers, having received a portion of the bounty that had been placed on Jesse James, soon left the state. The courthouse is still in use and the wooden bench the Fords sat on in court is still there.

The **Native American and History Gallery** (3406 Frederick Ave.; 816-232-8471) displays items from the more than four thousand artifacts in the Harry L. George Collection, considered one of the nation's best.

SEDALIA (PETTIS COUNTY)

The first wild and wooly cattle town in the Old West was not Abilene, Kansas. It was Sedalia, Missouri. Founded in 1857 along a feeder route to the Santa Fe Trail by George Rappeen Smith on the expectation that it would soon have a railroad connection, Sedalia was named for Smith's daughter Sarah, whose nickname was Sed.

The first Missouri Pacific train reached Sedalia in January 1861, but the Civil War interrupted any further railroad construction to the west. Still, by the fall of 1865 the railroad extended from St. Louis on the east to Kansas City on the west, via Sedalia. The town quickly boomed as Texas cattlemen began driving their herds from South Texas to the Sedalia rail yard, where they could be shipped to stockyards in Kansas City or to Chicago via St. Louis. An estimated 160,000 head of cattle moved through Sedalia in 1866 alone. In 1870 the Missouri, Kansas, and Texas Railroad (the Katy) also began serving Sedalia, furthering the town's growth. One of many families drawn to Sedalia in the 1880s because of its importance as a railroad center was that of young Scott Joplin, an African-American musician credited with later developing ragtime music.

"Move 'Em On, Head 'Em Up . . . !"

One of the more popular and longest-running Westerns during that genre's black-and-white television heyday was ***Rawhide***, a series built on the numerous challenges—from stampedes to cattle rustling—and interesting characters encountered by drovers pushing cattle up the trail from Texas to the railhead for shipment to eastern markets. Most viewers probably thought each trail drive's destination was Kansas, but trail boss Gil Favor (played by Eric Fleming), Rowdy Yates (Clint Eastwood), and the rest of the cast were always heading to Sedalia. The show was inspired by a diary kept in 1866 by real-life trail boss George C. Duffield who herded longhorn cattle from San Antonio to Sedalia. The first show aired January 9, 1959, and the series continued through 217 episodes until January 4, 1966.

The Sedalia Heritage Foundation maintains the old Missouri, Kansas, and Texas Railroad depot, built in 1896. Now known as the **Sedalia Katy Depot** (600 East 3rd St.; 660-826-2932), the ornate, two-and-a-half-story red brick and limestone train station handled passenger train traffic until 1958 and continued to see freight traffic until the Katy ceased operations in 1983. Acquired by the state in 1987, the facility was renovated and now serves as the town's welcome center. It also has exhibits related to Sedalia's railroad heritage.

Located in a former church, the **Pettis County Museum** (228 Dundee Ave.; 660-829-3102) also focuses on the area's history and culture. The Sedalia Commercial Historic District includes sixty-eight structures listed on the National Register of Historic Places.

SIBLEY (JACKSON COUNTY)

Under the supervision of Gen. William Clark, commander of the Lewis and Clark Expedition that set out to explore the northwest following the Louisiana Purchase, **Fort Osage** (105 Osage St.; 816-650-3278) was established at a strategic point on the Missouri River in 1808. First called Fort Clark, the name was changed to honor the Osage Indians, with whom the young nation was eager to have friendly relations.

Several reasons lay behind the building of the fort: The US wanted to make it plain to European powers that it had no intention of ever losing the vast territory it had purchased at a bargain price from France; secondly, the government was interested in peaceful interactions and trade with the Osage and other American Indian tribes; and thirdly, the garrison would serve as a gateway to western settlement.

The trade aspect was handled by George Sibley, for whom the town was later named. He ran a government-owned, three-and-one-half-story building known as a factory trade house. In this sense, "factory" was a legal term, not a place of manufacture. Sibley was the fort's "factor," in charge of recording the dollar value of exchanges. (Bowing to pressure from private trading companies, Congress got the US out of the trading post business in 1822.)

In 1825, Fort Osage was the point of departure for the party that surveyed the Santa Fe Trail. Two years later, the frontier having advanced, the fort was abandoned.

One hundred and fourteen years later, in 1941, Jackson County elected officials worked with historians and archeologists to fix the location of the long-vanished fort and reconstruct it. Beginning with one of the blockhouses and continuing over the years with the addition of the factory building, the other blockhouses, officer's quarters, troop barracks, and the stockade once intended to protect these structures, the process was completed in the 1960s. Fort Osage was designated as a National Historic Landmark in 1961.

Springfield (Greene County)
John Polk Campbell, a homesteader from Tennessee, made his claim on the land that would become Springfield in 1829, only eight years after Missouri statehood. Springfield was incorporated in 1838. Most accounts agree it was named for Springfield, Massachusetts, by an early settler who came from there.

When the Cherokee and other Southeastern American Indian tribes were forced from their homelands in 1838, the Indians and their military escort passed through Springfield on their journey to Indian Territory—an involuntary exodus later known as the Trail of Tears. The route they took from Springfield to Fort Smith, Arkansas, first known as the Military Road, became part of the Butterfield Overland Trail to California. In 1860 the telegraph line from St. Louis to Fort

Smith, a vital communication link, ran along the road, leading people to begin calling it the Telegraph or Wire Road. Now known as the Old Wire Road, the segment beginning in Springfield became part of one of the nation's most famous roadways, Route 66.

All on Account of a Pocket Watch

David Tutt seized Wild Bill Hickok's prized Waltham watch as collateral for a gambling debt, but Hickok's former friend was about to run out of time. Not wanting the whole town to know he'd lost his timepiece, Hickok told Tutt not to flaunt it. Tutt allowed as how he'd "pack that watch across the [square]" at high noon the next day. Hearing that, Hickok said Tutt had best not "pack that watch . . . unless dead men could walk."

It wasn't noon, but about 6:00 p.m. the next day when Tutt showed up on the square with two revolvers strapped to his hips. Packing as well, Hickok appeared and yelled at Tutt not to display the watch. Suddenly Tutt jerked one of his pistols from its holster and fired at Hickok. Wild Bill pulled his revolver at the same time. Tutt missed; Hickok did not. At roughly a hundred paces, Wild Bill had put a bullet through Tutt's heart.

The Wild West's first face-off, quick draw gunfight had just taken place. That duel-style of combat never caught on in the frontier, but did become a Hollywood staple.

Start your exploration of Springfield at the **Convention and Visitors Bureau** (815 East St. Louis St.; 417-881-5300).

The story of the historic Hickok-Tutt shootout is told in detail in Springfield's **History Museum on the Square** (157 Park Central Sq.; 417-831-1976), which opened in 2019. An engraved aluminum plaque in the southwest corner of **Park Central Square** offers an overview of the historic shootout and an audio tour of eight key locations connected to the fight is available.

Tutt's grave is in the northwest corner of **Maple Park Cemetery** (300 West Grand St.; 417-869-0217; lot 24, block 57).

STANTON (FRANKLIN COUNTY)

Even fake history can have a good story behind it. When researchers opened Jesse James's grave in 1995 to obtain a DNA sample to determine once and for all if the storied outlaw was really the person buried there, the results were unambiguous: The remains were those of Jesse James. No matter the historical truth, Stanton's **Jesse James Wax Museum** (exit 230, I-44; 573-927-5233), a tourist attraction dating to the 1940s, offers "evidence" supporting an alternative story. While the museum's website says it's up to visitors to be the judge, the exhibits focus on the hoary Wild West conspiracy theory that James staged his death and lived to a ripe old age as J. Frank Dalton.

Discovered in 1716, **Meramec Caverns** (1135 Highway W, Sullivan; 573-468-2283) in nearby Sullivan is a 4.6-mile scenic cavern system and popular tourist destination. But despite claims, there is no evidence Jesse James and his gang ever sought refuge inside.

WINSTON (DAVIESS COUNTY)

First called Croft's Crossing, Winston was laid out in 1871 as the Rock Island Railroad approached. However, when a post office opened a year later, it was named Winstonville to honor railroad official F. K. Winston. Seven years later the community was renamed Emporia but switched to Winston in 1889.

Turns Out Jesse James Wasn't Dead—Yet

Jesse James had been lying low. In fact, some believed he was dead. That theory arose with a newspaper report that the outlaw had been shot and killed by one of his own gang members near Galena, Kansas, in November 1879. As it turned out, James was alive and well. On July 15, 1881, he, his brother Frank, and three associates bought tickets and boarded a Chicago, Rock Island, and Pacific Railroad train at the Winston depot. After the train left the station, James fired several shots to call attention to the fact that he and his men were taking over the train. At just the wrong moment, Conductor William Harrison Westfall (1843–1881) happened to stand up after collecting a ticket and one of James's bullets hit the hapless railroad man. Dying, he staggered to the car door and either fell or was pushed off the train. Another of James's wild shots hit and killed passenger Frank McMillan (1853–1881). The outlaw later said he regretted the accidental killings. But when a newspaper reported that Westfall had been conductor on the special train that carried the two Pinkerton detectives who bombed his mother's house (*see* Kearney, Missouri), James told his cousin he was glad it happened. The robbers easily eluded a sheriff's posse after the holdup.

The 1871-vintage **Rock Island Depot** in Winston (Highway 69 and Route Y) stood abandoned for years. Later it was used as a city storage shed until the Winston Historical Society restored it in 1989 for use as a museum.

Slain conductor Westfall, who left behind a wife and four children, is buried in the **Old Plattsburg Cemetery** in Clinton County, Missouri. The other robbery victim, McMillen, is buried in **Oakdale Cemetery** in Wilton, Iowa.

IOWA

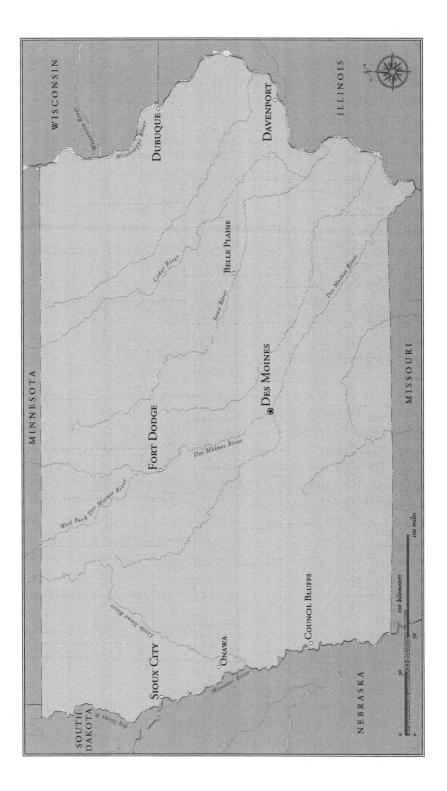

ADAIR (GUTHRIE COUNTY)

First known as Summit Cut, the Adair community began when the Chicago, Rock Island, and Pacific Railroad laid tracks through Iowa in 1868. When the town was incorporated in 1872 it was named Adair for Gen. John Adair, who served in the War of 1812 and later was elected governor of Kentucky.

Jesse James Enters the Train-Robbing Business

Just west of town on a sharp curb near the Turkey Creek bridge, on July 21, 1873, bandits derailed a Rock Island line locomotive pulling five coaches, two sleepers, and an express car. John Rafferty, the train's thirty-year-old engineer, died in the crash.

While the record is clear enough on what transpired that night, whether the holdup was the first train robbery west of the Mississippi or merely one of the first is debatable. (The first train robbery in the East took place in 1866.) One thing is unquestioned: The perpetrators of the Iowa crime were Jesse James and his brother, Frank; Cole, Jim, and Tom Younger; Clell Miller; and Bill Chadwell. All would be heard from again.

James and his men forced express car guard John Burgess to open the safe and collected roughly $2,000. The robbers also took an additional $1,000 in cash and valuables from passengers, but the huge shipment of gold that was their real target turned out to have been on a different train.

Though only one person died in the robbery, it could have been much worse. When he first spotted the pulled track, engineer Rafferty threw the train into reverse and applied the air brakes. That slowed the train enough to prevent widespread injuries among the crew and the one hundred passengers.

After the robbers fled, railroad worker Levi Clay walked to Casey, where the telegrapher at the depot there spread word of the crime to Des Moines and Omaha. When the news reached Council Bluffs, a train full of armed men left for Adair, dropping detachments along the way where saddled horses awaited them. The outlaws succeeded in making it to Missouri, where friends sheltered them.

Donated by the Rock Island Railroad in 1954, an upright drive wheel from an old steam locomotive and a section of track mark the **robbery site** (1156 Anita-Adair Rd.), one and a half miles west of Adair and a half mile south of I-80. A modern-day outlaw stole the bronze plaque from the wheel in 1974, but it was later recovered in Ohio when the thief's house burned down. Discovered in the charred debris, the plaque was returned to the robbery site. Holdup victim John Rafferty is buried in **Saint Mary's Cemetery** (467-473 South 18th St., Clinton).

Albert City (Buena Vista County)

Founded in 1890 by George Anderson, the town was first known as Mantorp for a small farming community in Sweden. However, near the new Iowa town was a community called Marathon. Postal officials feared the two "M" towns would lead to misdirected mail, so they rejected Mantorp as a post office name. Accordingly, the new town was renamed for Anderson's wife, Albertina. By the turn of the century, Albert had grown large enough for incorporation.

On November 16, 1901, Albert City marshal Charles J.E. Lodine (1868–1901) received a telegram informing him that the bank in Greenville, Iowa, had been burglarized the night before by three men believed to be headed his way. Not long after, someone reported that three strangers were eating at the depot. Believing the trio were likely the wanted men, the marshal recruited a posse and went to arrest them. But, when he yelled, "You are our prisoners!" the three yeggs pulled handguns and opened fire on the lawman and deputized citizens. The subsequent gun battle left the marshal and posse member John Lund-blad (1871–1901) mortally wounded. The posse also gravely wounded one of the suspects, but the other two escaped. All three combatants later died, with the two escaped suspects soon arrested after a second shootout in a cornfield near Laurens, Iowa. Roughly sixty shots had been fired in the Albert City battle.

The gunfight took place in and around the Chicago, Milwaukee, St. Paul, and Pacific Railroad depot, a wood-frame building with a two-story section. In 1977 the discontinued depot was in danger of being razed to make room for a grain elevator, but the town of Albert and the local historical society bought the 1899-vintage depot and moved it to its current location for use as a museum. The **Albert City Historical Museum** (212 2nd St. South; 712-843-5684) has a pistol used by one of the burglary suspects and several score empty shell casings picked up after the shootout. Starker evidence of the battle are five bullet holes still visible in the north wall of the old depot.

Swedish-born Marshal Charles Lodine lies in the Lodine family plot in **Fairfield Cemetery** (GPS coordinates: N42° 46.70', W94° 58.15'). Johan August (John) Lundblad is also in the cemetery, which is due west of Albert on the north side of 510th Street, a continuation of Highway Street.

The mortally wounded outlaw was never identified—not that law enforcement officials tried very hard. He was dead and as far as most folks were concerned, that was good enough. His remains were laid in a plain pine box and promptly buried. At some later point, a small granite marker was placed over the grave. All it says is: "Bank Robber/ Nov. 21, 1901." That's a slight libel of the late criminal—while rob-bery and burglary both are felonies, breaking into a bank at night is not the same as robbing it at gunpoint in broad daylight.

ANAMOSA (JONES COUNTY)

Settlers first came to this area along the Wapsipinicon River in 1838, calling their community Buffalo Forks. But when the town was incor-porated in 1856, it was as Lexington. There being too many places with that name, postal officials insisted on something else. What someone came up with was the much more evocative Anamosa, believed to be the name of a young Indian girl of whom some of the early residents had become fond.

In 1872 state officials decided Iowa needed a second penitentiary and chose Anamosa as the site. Most Old West prisons were drab affairs, ascetic considerations ignored in favor of sturdy if low-cost architecture. But not the new lockup at Anamosa. Designed by architect L. W. Forest and built with locally quarried limestone, the Italianate-style prison looks more like a castle than a penal institution. Known for a time as "The White Palace of the West," it remains in use.

Outside the walls, in a stone building originally used as a barn and for inmate labor cheese making, is the **Anamosa State Penitentiary Museum** (406 North High St.; 319-462-3504), which documents the construction of the facility, its history, and its more notorious inmates—people such as Charles Knox Pope Wells.

Born in Missouri in 1851, **Pope Wells** (as he was best known) was a bank and train robber who claimed to have fought Indians with Kit Carson and ridden with the Jesse James and Cole Young gang for a time. It was also said he'd killed thirty men. While that's way exaggerated, he did get convicted of murder in 1882 and sentenced to life in the Iowa State Prison at Fort Madison. That crime occurred during an escape attempt when he was already in prison for robbery. Wells and two other inmates used chloroform to disable a guard and he later died from too strong a dose. Described as well-spoken and intelligent, Wells wrote an autobiography, *The Life and Adventures of Polk Wells*, while in prison. He did most of his time at the prison in Fort Madison, but in 1896 was transferred to Anamosa. Suffering from tuberculosis, he died there sixteen days later. There's a grave marker in the prison cemetery with "C. Wells 1896" engraved on it, but his body was returned to Missouri where it was turned over to a medical school for dissection.

ARNOLD'S PARK (DICKINSON COUNTY)

What thirteen-year-old Abbie Gardner and her family went through, while similar to what happened to others again and again across the Wild West, is slightly different. In what came to be called the **Spirit Lake Massacre**, on March 8, 1857, Dakota Indians under Inkpaduta killed thirty-three settlers in the vicinity of Lake Okoboji. The warriors took Abbie and three other women as captives. After eighty-four hellish days Abbie was rescued. Unlike many whites taken by Indians, though never totally the same afterward, she managed to readjust to an extent. At fourteen, she married eighteen-year-old Casville Sharp and went on to have three children.

In 1883 she published a book on her harrowing experiences, *History of the Spirit Lake Massacre and Captivity of Miss Abbie Gardner*. Again, numerous other captives had done that, but what she did with the money derived from sales of her book, which went through seven editions, is unique in frontier history. First, in 1891, she purchased thirteen acres her slain family had once owned, including the log cabin where she had been captured and her family killed. Then, she turned the cabin into one of the Wild West's first history-related tourist attractions. For a quarter (only a dime for children) visitors could see exhibits inside the cabin. In 1893 she began lobbying the state legislature to fund the erection of a monument at the site of the massacre. Lawmakers appropriated $5,000 in 1894 and the monument was dedicated on July 26, 1895, before a crowd of seven thousand. The remains of massacre victims that could be found in the area were placed in a common grave beneath the monument. Abbie Gardner Sharp died on January 17, 1921, at the age of seventy-eight and was buried with her birth family near their old cabin. The former captive had been able to do what many victims of Indian captivity could not—she forgave her captors. As one of the markers at her grave attests:

ABIGAIL GARDNER SHARP... LIVED TO EMBRACE IN CHRISTIAN BENEVOLENCE THE AMERICAN INDIAN AND ALL MANKIND.

The restored Gardner cabin and museum still stands at **Abbie Gardner State Historic Site** (74 Monument Dr.; 712-332-7248) near the town of Arnold. The 1895 monument and mass grave of the victims is also on the site. The separate **Gardner Family Cemetery** is nearby. **Pillsbury Point State Park** (23 Prairie Ln.) preserves the massacre site.

BELLE PLAINE (BENTON COUNTY)

French for "beautiful plain," Belle Plaine was founded in 1862 with the approach of the first transcontinental railroad. Seven years before the town was platted, Robert and Margaret McLaury and their growing brood of children came to the area from New York state.

Robert farmed, practiced law, and fathered more children. When his wife died in 1857, he soon remarried and continued to expand the family. In 1878 two of his boys, Frank and his younger brother Tom, decided to head west to Arizona Territory. They established a cattle ranch not far from a then-booming mining town called Tombstone. There, on October 26, 1881, Frank and Tom died in the shootout that became world-famous as the Gunfight at the OK Corral. (Brother Will followed in his father's law-abiding footsteps and later was a judge in Fort Worth, Texas.) Ironically enough, the man who had a hand in the violent demise of Frank and Tom also spent a good part of his childhood in Iowa, only sixty miles from Belle Plaine (see Pellum, Iowa).

The McLaury family farm was west of Belle Plaine, just north of what is now Highway E66. The **Bell Plaine Area Museum** (901 12th St.; 319-434-6093) tells the story of the town. Margaret McLaury, who died of typhoid, is buried in **Wright Cemetery** (GPS coordinates: N41° 54.82', W92° 15.86'), a small rural cemetery outside Belle Plaine. One of her sons, Edmond, who died from health issues related to his imprisonment for a time during the Civil War, is also buried here.

Bellevue (Jackson County)

One of the Wild West's earlier instances of vigilantism occurred in Bellevue, but with a twist.

Founded in 1835 by John D. Bell and named county seat two years later, Bellevue soon became a busy riverboat town with thriving local businesses. One of those businesses was the two-story log hotel W. W. Brown owned. Not feeling morally constrained to limit his income to honestly earned money, Brown formed a gang of thieves and counterfeiters.

On April 1, 1840, a posse led by the county sheriff, who had arrest warrants for Brown and his men, stormed the hotel. That precipitated a shooting that left Brown and two of his henchmen dead. The posse lost four of their own but succeeded in taking custody of thirteen of the wanted men.

This is where what happened varied from the norm. Generally, once a vigilante group determined that action needed to be taken, the law breakers ended up at the end of a rope. But the good citizens of Bellevue were divided as to what course to follow. Some wanted to hang their prisoners, others favored the laying on of lashes. Finally, the posse decided to rely on one of the mainstays of democracy—a vote.

When the vote was tabulated, the majority favored merely whipping the surviving gang members. That punishment meted out, the vigilantes placed the undesirables on a flatbottom boat, provided three days' worth of provisions, and watched from the landing until the vessel drifted down river.

The hotel where the battle took place no longer stands, but a stone marker detailing the incident is in a city park (400 block of Riverview Drive) overlooking the Mississippi. The **Young Historical Museum** (406 North Riverview Dr.; 563-872-3794) tells the town's story. It is named for Albert Young, who provided in his will that his Gothic Revival home be donated for use as a local museum.

BURR OAK (WINNESHIEK COUNTY)

Platted in 1855, Burr Oak is a small town just south of the Minnesota border. In 1876, Charles and Caroline Ingalls moved their family—including future best-selling *Little House on the Prairie* series author Laura Ingalls Wilder—from Walnut Grove, Minnesota, to Burr Oak. Having lost two years of crops to grasshoppers, the Ingalls relocated because Charles had agreed to help family friend William Steadman manage the Masters Hotel there.

The Ingalls lived in the hotel, but the situation there did not work out and the family moved to rented space near one of the town's saloons. That did not prove conducive to family life, so Charles moved his brood to a small brick house outside of town until he decided he'd had enough of Burr Oak and moved back to Minnesota for a time.

Most of the places the Ingalls family lived later figured in Wilder's children's books, but she did not write of her time spent in Burr Oak.

The old hotel still stands, has been restored, and now accommodates the **Laura Ingalls Wilder Museum** (3603 236th Ave.; 563-735-5916).

CORYDON (WAYNE COUNTY)

When Wayne County was being organized, the county judge took it upon himself to name the county seat Corydon—the name of his hometown in Indiana. The Iowa incarnation of Corydon was laid out in 1851 and while it's still a small town, it continues as county seat.

Twenty years after its founding, on June 3, 1871, almost everyone in Corydon turned out to hear noted orator Henry Clay Dean speak outside the Methodist church. Dean, a man Mark Twain called "a volcano" who could draw a crowd of farmers from fifty miles around, was with great animation holding his audience spellbound when four horsemen galloped up. "We robbed the bank, catch us if you can," one of them yelled, holding up the loot for everyone to see. But the crowd took the young men for pranksters and returned their attention to Dean. Cursing the "damned Yankees," the men rode off on their way back to Missouri. Only later, when someone happened to walk into the bank and find the cashier had been tied up and the safe emptied, did townspeople realize the man who interrupted Dean had not been kidding. A posse mounted up to pursue the robbers but didn't catch them. Later it was established that the men who pulled off the holdup were Jesse and Frank James, Clell Miller, and Cole Younger.

The bank where the robbery occurred was a wood-frame building that no longer stands, but the **Prairie Trails Museum** (515 East Jefferson St.; 641-872-2211) has an exhibit devoted to the robbery that features a photograph of the bank. A more tangible part of the display is the safe that had been in the bank when the robbery occurred. The Wayne County Historical Society's archival holdings include a letter that contains a first-hand account of the holdup.

COUNCIL BLUFFS (POTTAWATTAMIE COUNTY)

On their way to the Pacific Northwest, in 1804 Meriwether Lewis and Capt. William Clark held a council with members of the Otoe Tribe at a bend in the Missouri River about ten miles north of its confluence with the Platte River. After that, the area became known as Council Bluff (singular). In 1837, relocated from the Great Lakes area by several treaties, the Pottawattamie people came to western Iowa and established a village at Council Bluff. In 1846 a party of Mormons on their way from Illinois to Utah spent the winter at Council Bluff, though some remained across the river where Omaha later developed. Some of the Mormons decided to stay a while and formed a community called Kanesville. Meanwhile, in 1848, the Pottawattamie were moved farther west to Kansas. The remainder of the Mormons left Council Bluff in 1852. A year later the town was becoming a busy jumping off place for western travelers, and the name was changed to Council Bluffs (plural).

Many of the Wild West sites around Council Bluffs are directly tied to the city's importance as a gateway to the American West. Since 1911 a tall granite obelisk (western end of Lafayette Avenue) has stood on a bluff overlooking the Missouri River valley. The **Lincoln**

Monument honors Abraham Lincoln, not for his leadership during the Civil War or the Emancipation Proclamation, but for the decision he reached while standing at this spot in 1859. The future president had eaten lunch with **Grenville M. Dodge** (1831–1916) at Council Bluffs' Pacific Hotel. Over their meal Lincoln asked Dodge for his opinion on the route the nation's first transcontinental railroad should take. Dodge recommended extending the route through the Platte River valley with Council Bluffs as the starting place. Lincoln strongly advocated a railroad that would connect the East and West Coasts, and after he gained the White House, despite his preoccupation with keeping the nation united in another, much more urgent way, he signed into law the **Pacific Railway Act**. The president also issued an executive order naming Council Bluffs the eastern terminus of the planned railroad, a line that would become the Union Pacific.

As chief engineer for the Union Pacific, Dodge was a key figure in the building of the first transcontinental railroad and the namesake of Dodge City, a once-rowdy Kansas cattle town now known worldwide. He is the man on the right shaking hands with Samuel S. Montague in one of the nation's most iconic photographs, the May 10, 1869, ceremony marking the completion of the rail line linking the east and west coasts.

A Union major general in the Civil War and presidential confidant, Dodge later engaged in the mercantile business, organized a bank, surveyed the Missouri River valley for the transcontinental railroad, and served in the US Congress.

Dodge built an elegant Victorian home in Council Bluffs in 1869. It cost $35,000, a huge amount at the time. Designed by Chicago architect William Boyington, the fourteen-room, three-story mansion stands on a high terrace overlooking the Missouri valley. The house featured parquet floors; cherry, walnut, and butternut woodwork; and several avant-garde conveniences, including central heating and hot and cold running water.

Following Dodge's death in 1916, his family retained ownership of the house until 1943. The house was offered to various groups in

1949, but none were interested, so the contents were auctioned for $15,000. The new owner transformed the property into a boarding house. In 1961 the house was designated as a National Historic Landmark. Two years later, the Pottawattamie County Historical Society led an effort to acquire the home and it was purchased for $30,000 in 1964. After restoration, it opened to visitors in 1965.

Maintained by a nonprofit foundation, the **Dodge House** (605 3rd St.; 712-322-2406) is open to the public. Dodge is buried in **Walnut Hill Cemetery** (1350 East Pierce St.).

Squirrel Cage Jail

Most surviving Wild West–era jails are more noted for the infamous prisoners they held than for their architecture. But the old Pottawattamie County lockup, known as the **Squirrel Cage Jail** (226 Pearl St.), is one of only three jails in the nation with a particularly unique design: A cylindrical three-story revolving steel cage with ten pie-shaped cells on each level. Inside a more traditional four-sided barred enclosure on the first floor, the forty-five-ton cage slowly rotated so that a jailer sitting in the hub of the lazy Susan–like hoosegow could keep an eye on every prisoner. Built for $30,000 in 1885, the unusual jail continued in use until 1969. The old building went to the Council Bluffs Park Department, was listed on the National Register of Historic Places in 1972, and was restored in 1977. The Pottawattamie County Historical Society (712-323-2509) maintains a museum there and provides tours.

Opened May 10, 2003—the 134th anniversary of the completion of the transcontinental railroad—the **Union Pacific Railroad Museum** (200 Pearl St.; 712-329-8307) tells the dramatic story of the railroad line that worked its way westward from Council Bluffs to connect with the Central Pacific's east-bound tracks. The museum occupies the 1905-vintage brick, Beaux arts–style former Carnegie Public Library.

The **Western Historic Trails Center** (3434 Richard Downing Ave.; 712-366-4900) tells the stories of the Lewis and Clark Expedition, the Oregon, California, and Mormon Trails. All passed through Iowa.

World's Largest Golden Spike

In time, even Wild West–themed tourist attractions transcend their phoniness to become historic. That's the case with the fifty-six-foot reinforced concrete replica of the famous golden spike driven when the Union Pacific Railroad finally met the Central Pacific Railroad in May 1869. Seventy years later, famed director Cecil B. DeMille produced an epic film called *Union Pacific* that told the story about the building of the railroad that connected the nation. Starring Barbara Stanwick and Joel McCrea, the movie premiered simultaneously at three different theaters across the Missouri River from Council Bluffs to Omaha, Nebraska.

Despite Council Bluffs's significant role in the real story, Omaha got all the attention when Hollywood came to town for the film's opening. Hoping for at least some recognition, Council Bluffs built the towering spike and covered it with gold glitter. At its base went a plaque reading: "Eastern Terminus of the Union Pacific Railroad Fixed by Abraham Lincoln."

DeMille spoke at the statue's April 28, 1939, dedication and predicted it would stand a hundred years. The monument is not in the best part of downtown, but visitors interested in oddball attractions still come by for photo ops. The spike is on the south side of the railroad tracks (2073 9th Ave.), just east of where the avenue intersects South 21st Street.

DAVENPORT (SCOTT COUNTY)

On his epic exploration of the Louisiana Purchase land, US Army Lt. Zebulon Pike camped at the future location of Davenport on August 27, 1805. French Canadian trapper and trader Antoine Le Claire founded Davenport on May 14, 1836, naming it for his friend Col. George Davenport, who had been stationed at nearby Fort Armstrong during the 1832 Black Hawk War. The city was incorporated in 1839.

Davenport grew as a riverboat port, but it was another form of transportation that stimulated further development—the Rock Island Railroad. The line built the first railroad bridge across the Mississippi River in 1856, linking Davenport to Rock Island, Illinois, and from there to Chicago. Davenport became a thriving railroad hub.

Businessmen in Davenport were jubilant that their community had a rail connection, but steamboat owners correctly realized that their way of making a living would be sinking as sure as a sternwheeler hitting a large, sunken snag. On May 6, 1856, the master of the steamboat *Effie Afton* "accidentally" crashed his vessel into the newly dedicated span. Whether it was an accident or not, the *Effie Afton*'s owner filed suit against the railroad. An Illinois lawyer named Abraham Lincoln represented the railroad in a case that went all the way to the US Supreme Court. The court ruled that a railroad company did have the right to build a bridge to extend its service.

The **Putnam Museum** (1717 West 12th St.; 563-324-1933) interprets the history of Davenport and the Quad Cities area.

DES MOINES (POLK COUNTY)

When US Army Capt. James Allen oversaw construction in 1843 of a post at the junction of the Des Moines and Raccoon Rivers, he suggested—presumably with a straight face—that it be named Fort Raccoon. Fortunately for the city of Des Moines, which later took its name from the fort, when Allen's proposal reached Washington, the US War Department nixed the suggestion. Whether the officer's second choice was to name the fort after the other river that flowed near it, or was someone else's idea, the military brass went with Des Moines.

The army abandoned the post in 1846, but the small community that had grown around it remained. By 1851 the town had been incorporated and six years later shortened its name from Fort Des Moines to Des Moines. The same year, Iowa City lost its status as capital and the seat of state government moved to Des Moines. Despite its status as capital city, Des Moines grew slowly until after the Civil War when it gained a railroad connection. From that point, Des Moines experienced rapid growth, becoming Iowa's largest city.

Polk County has more than ninety properties listed on the National Register of Historic Places, including the 1874 **Iowa State Capitol** (East 9th Street and Grand Avenue).

Fort Des Moines's log buildings did not survive, but archeologists determined that foundations from structures at the fort are covered by pavement in the area of Martin Luther King Jr. Parkway and 1st Street. In 1901, at a different location, the army opened a new Fort Des Moines that continued in operation until after World War II. The **Fort Des Moines Museum and Education Center** (75 East Army Post Rd.; 515-400-3678) has exhibits on the second post's role as the army's first training center for black officers.

The **State Historical Museum** (600 East Locust St.; 515-281-1111) is operated by the State Historical Society of Iowa, an entity founded in 1857 that is itself historic. Housed in a building constructed in 1899 (and later enlarged), the museum has more than eighty thousand artifacts related to Iowa history.

Des Moines also has the **Wells Fargo Museum** (666 Walnut St.; 515-245-8400), part of the network of Wells Fargo–operated museums dedicated to the history of the corporation's stagecoach and express car era.

DUBUQUE (DUBUQUE COUNTY)

Iowa's oldest city, Dubuque is named for Julien Dubuque, a French-Canadian trader who settled in the area in 1785, building a cabin on a bluff above the Mississippi River where the city would later be founded. Dubuque won the trust of the local Meskwaki (Fox) Tribe, who had been gathering and smelting lead ore along the river for several decades and gained their permission to do his own mining in the area. Spain, which then claimed much of the land west of the

Mississippi, granted Dubuque 1,380 acres designated as the Mines of Spain. The pioneer operated a trading post and continued his mining operations until his death in 1810, seven years after the Louisiana Purchase gave the young US control of 827,000 square miles west of the Mississippi.

Chartered in 1833, the city of Dubuque lay in unorganized US territory until the creation of Iowa Territory in 1838. When the lead mines in the area played out, Dubuque survived as riverboat port, milling town, and industrial center.

Still standing in Dubuque is a 120-foot stone and brick **shot tower** (Commercial Street and the river front) built in 1856 for the manufacture of lead pellets for muzzle-loading shotguns. To form the small projectiles, workers poured molten lead through plates penetrated with holes of various gauges. The droplets rounded as they then fell into water vats to cool and solidify. After the Civil War, the tower was converted into a watch tower for fires in the lumber yards. Listed on the National Register, the structure is one of the few remaining shot towers in the nation.

Another tower, a round, twenty-five-foot stone monument erected in 1897, marks the supposed burial place of Dubuque, his Indian wife Potosa, and her father Peosta. The monument, a National Historic Landmark, is now part of **Mines of Spain State Recreation Area** (8991 Bellevue Heights; 563-556-0620).

The history, culture, and animal life of the river that played such an important part in the settlement of the West is the focus of the **National Mississippi River Museum and Aquarium** (350 East 3rd St.; 563-557-9545). A Smithsonian Museum affiliate, it is the nation's largest museum devoted to the river.

FORT ATKINSON (WINNESHIEK COUNTY)

Most military posts in the West were established to protect travelers and settlers from American Indians angered by the loss of their land, but in 1840 Fort Atkinson was built to keep two tribes from fighting each other.

That would seem like a simple enough objective, but the situation was complicated—just one example of the US government's patchwork and often unsuccessful efforts to acquire land from American Indians with some degree of equity. In 1825 the government had established a 200-mile-long boundary line between land occupied by the Dakota Sioux to the north and the Sac and Fox Tribes on the south. But the imaginary border meant nothing to the two warring factions, so the government carved out a forty-mile-wide neutral zone. Into that zone, the government would be moving the Winnebago people from their land in Wisconsin as human buffers.

To make the deal look more attractive, the US offered the Winnebago money and military protection. To that end, construction began on a substantial post with two dozen stone buildings surrounded by a nearly twelve-foot-high wooden stockade. The army named the post for Gen. Henry Atkinson, commander of the Sixth Infantry.

Fort Atkinson took two years to build, but before the end of the decade, it was abandoned. With more and more settlers coming to Iowa, the Indians had been moved farther west. The government property was sold at auction in 1855 and the buyer platted the town of Fort Atkinson on the former military land. In 1921 the ruins of the old fort were acquired by the state and are now part of **Fort Atkinson State Preserve** (303 2nd St. Northwest; 563-425-4161).

FORT DODGE (WEBSTER COUNTY)

The city of Fort Dodge grew from a frontier military installation by the same name, something that would happen again in Kansas some years later when another Fort Dodge led to the founding of Dodge City. But the posts were not active at the same time, and each honored a different man.

Fort Dodge, Iowa, was established in 1850 on the Des Moines River at its juncture with Lizard Creek in what is now Webster County to protect settlers from the Sioux. Originally named Fort Clarke, the post was renamed for US Senator Henry Dodge of Wisconsin, who had fought in the Black Hawk War. When the fort was abandoned in 1853, William Williams purchased the land and the post's buildings and had a townsite laid out. The history of the old fort and the city that retained its name is the focus of the **Fort Museum and Frontier Village** (1 Museum Rd.; 515-573-4231). The complex includes a replica of the old fort and a collection of restored vintage buildings representative of an Old West town. The museum has an exhibit on what is now known as the **Dragoon Trail**, the 200-mile route that mounted US infantrymen called Dragoons (the forerunner of the US Cavalry) took in the summer of 1835 from present Des Moines to what later became Fort Dodge. The state has a series of nine historical markers along the route, which roughly paralleled the Des Moines, Boone, and Raccoon Rivers. The leader of the expedition was Col. Stephen W. Kearny, who went on to participate in the 1846–1848 war with Mexico that opened the American Southwest.

Initially an agricultural center, Fort Dodge's economy was later bolstered with the development of gypsum mining in the area. That operation would figure in one of the nation's more famous hoaxes.

Just a Block of Gypsum . . . Until

In 1868 a man named George Hull bought a block of gypsum quarried near Fort Dodge—falsely claiming he intended to produce a statue of Abraham Lincoln—and had it shipped to Chicago. There, he paid to have it carved into human form. The ten-foot piece was then shipped to Hull in Binghamton, New York. From there, he took it to his cousin's farm near Cardiff, New York, and buried it. The following year two unsuspecting well diggers found it and when word got out, newspapers played it as the discovery of a large, petrified prehistoric man. Headlines referred to him as the **Cardiff Giant**. Hull did not want to deprive the public of the pleasure of seeing the big guy, so he put it on display and charged people for the privilege of viewing the creature first-hand. Knowing a good scam when he saw it,

P.T. Barnham tried to buy the sculpture, but Hull wouldn't sell. Accordingly, Barnham had his own man carved and put it on exhibition. Hull sued but lost. The Fort Museum and Frontier Village has a replica of the giant.

FORT MADISON (LEE COUNTY)

Fort Madison the town developed around the early-day military installation named for President James Madison.

The fort was one of three posts the army planned to establish following congressional ratification of the 1803 Louisiana Purchase. Built in 1808, Fort Madison was a collection of one-story log buildings surrounded by a stockade and protected by a two-level blockhouse. Located on the west bank of the upper Mississippi River, it was established thirty years before Iowa became a territory and thirty-eight years before it became a state. During the War of 1812, American Indians allied with the British laid siege to the fort, but the garrison held. The Indians attacked the fort again in the summer of 1813. This time, the ranking officer realized the Indians would likely overrun the post, so he ordered that it be torched and escaped downriver in boats. Though Fort Madison pre-dated the Wild West era by forty years, it is notable in that its establishment marked the beginning of the long cultural clash between American Indians and Euro-Americans west of the Mississippi. Also, it was the first American military post in the West to be attacked by Indians. The reconstructed Fort Madison (716 Riverview Dr.; 319-372-6318) houses an interpretive museum.

In 1839 the **Iowa State Prison**, modeled after a penitentiary in Auburn, New York, was built in Fort Madison. Remodeled in 1982 the prison continued in use until the state opened a new facility in 2015. The old stone prison (449 1st St.), opened when the US was only fifty-seven years old and consisted of only twenty-six states, is still maintained by the state. However, a nonprofit foundation is working to develop it as a historic site. **Historic Iowa State Penitentiary, Inc.** (319-372-5432) periodically offers guided tours of the old lockup.

Le Claire (Scott County)

Named for French Canadian trader Antoine Le Claire, the town was incorporated in 1855 though settlement at this point along the Mississippi River had begun in the 1830s.

Newly married, Isaac Cody and his wife Mary left Ohio for Iowa Territory in 1840. To get there, they traveled down the Ohio River from Cincinnati and then up the Mississippi to Davenport where Cody opened a trading post. A year later, the couple moved to the riverboat town of Le Claire. On February 26, 1846, in a log cabin a few miles outside of town, Mary gave birth to a son the couple named William Frederick. Young Cody spent the first nine years of his life in and around Le Claire before his father decided to relocate to Kansas Territory. In April 1854, the Cody family left in a wagon for Leavenworth.

The **Buffalo Bill Museum** (199 North Front St.; 563-289-5580), has exhibits on William "Buffalo Bill" Cody as well as on the general history of Le Claire and Scott County.

Two miles north of town off North Cody Road is an Iowa historical marker at the site of **Cody's boyhood home**, the house his family lived in from 1847 to 1853. The two-story wood-frame house stood at that location until 1930 when the Chicago, Burlington, and Quincy Railroad moved it to the Buffalo Bill Cody Center of the West in Cody, Wyoming.

A historical marker stands at the site of the log cabin where Cody was born (northwest corner of Territorial Road and 23rd Street).

The Cody family also lived for a time in Princeton in a two-story stone house, later enlarged by a subsequent owner, known today as the **Buffalo Bill Cody Homestead** (28050 230th Ave., Princeton; 563-225-2981).

The *Lone Star*

Likely named for Texas, the *Lone Star* is the oldest surviving wooden-hulled steamboat in the West. Now the most popular feature of the Buffalo Bill Museum, she was built in Lyons, Iowa, in 1869 and in one configuration or another, continued in operation on the Mississippi for just shy of a century. Originally a wood-fired sidewheeler that operated as a passenger and mail-carrying packet, in 1890 she was reconfigured as a sternwheeler for use as a towboat. Another refitting came in 1899, followed by a final redo in 1922, when the boat was converted into a dredge. The *Lone Star* remained in use until the spring of 1968. She was designated as a National Historic Landmark in 1989. At first dry-docked outside the museum, in 2008 the *Lone Star* was enclosed in a glass-and-steel addition.

MISSOURI VALLEY (HARRISON COUNTY)

Missouri Valley was platted in 1867 when the Chicago and North Western Railroad was laying tracks across Iowa. Two additional rail lines later served Missouri Valley and it became a busy rail center. At one point, twenty-five passenger trains a day stopped there.

Before the railroads came to Iowa, steamboats plying the Missouri River carried people and goods. On April 1, 1865, while churning upstream laden with supplies intended for the goldfields in Montana, the steamboat *Bertrand* hit a submerged log and sank. The boat's owners salvaged what they could, but most of the vessel's cargo was written off. One hundred and four years later, treasure hunters relying on historical records and electronic detection devices located the wreck, which had been buried beneath some thirty feet of silt. The discovery occurred on the **DeSoto National Wildlife Refuge** (1434 316th Ln.; 712-388-4800), so under federal law, anything recovered from the site belonged to the government. The finders went on to excavate the site, removing some quarter million artifacts ranging from well-preserved clothing to tools and food items. A representative sampling of the artifacts is displayed in a museum at the refuge maintained by the US Fish and Wildlife Service.

ONAWA (MONONA COUNTY)

Named for a feminine character mentioned in Henry Wadsworth Longfellow's 1855 epic poem *The Song of Hiawatha*, Onawa was platted in 1857. The townsite included what still stands as the widest Main Street in the nation. Long before the first settlers arrived in this part of western Iowa, the Lewis and Clark Expedition spent the night near here on August 9, 1804.

Opened in 1924, the 176-acre **Lewis and Clark State Park** (21914 Park Loop; 712-423-2829) features two replicas of the fifty-five-foot keel boat in which the explorers made their way up the Missouri River. One of the boats is used on Blue Lake, an oxbow lake created when the river changed its course. The other replica is on display in the park's visitor center. Built in 1985, the boat was used in the 1997 PBS documentary on Lewis and Clark, *Undaunted Courage.* The interpretive center, opened in 2013, also has full-size replicas of the smaller boats the expedition used on the return leg of their journey.

PELLA (MARION COUNTY)

Led by Henry Peter Scholte, Dutch immigrants escaping famine and religious persecution in the Netherlands founded Pella in 1847. Even before they left Europe, the immigrants decided to name their new home Pella, or City of Refuge. After reaching the US, the group settled between the Skunk and Des Moines Rivers in Marion County. There they purchased eighteen thousand acres of fertile farmland for around $1.25 per acre, the beginning of Pella. Though best known for its tulips and Dutch windmills, Pella has a connection with one of the Wild West's most famous figures.

Wyatt Earp's Boyhood Home

Nicholas and Virginia Earp came to Iowa in 1850 to farm 160 acres northeast of Pella granted to Nicholas for his military service during the Mexican War. Earp's growing family included young Wyatt Berry Stapp Earp, born March 19, 1848, in Monmouth, Illinois.

The Earp clan spent fourteen years in Pella, where Wyatt's brothers Warren and Morgan were born. The family left Iowa in 1864 for California. Though their farm lay a few miles outside of town, the Earps lived in a two-story brick row house built by brothers B. H. and J. H. H. Van Spanckeren, two of the original settlers. Restored to its 1850s appearance in 1966, the **Wyatt Earp Boyhood Home** (505–507 Franklin St.) was listed on the National Register of Historic Places in 1990. It is one of twenty-four structures of the **Pella Historical Village** (641-620-9463), a museum complex operated by the Pella Historical Society. For more on local attractions, check with the **Pella Visitor Center** (815 Broadway St., Ste. 1; 641-204-0885).

SIOUX CITY (WOODBURY AND PLYMOUTH COUNTIES)

The point on the Missouri River between the mouths of the lesser Big Sioux and Floyd Rivers that would become Sioux City was first visited by French fur trappers in the 1700s, though it was not platted until 1854. Named for the Yankton Sioux, the town became an important waypoint for western travelers and a busy riverboat landing. After gaining a rail connection in 1868, the town enjoyed further prosperity.

Sergeant Floyd

They trekked across a virtually unexplored territory, navigating dangerous waterways, traversing rugged terrain, and interacting with native peoples, but over the course of the twenty-eight-month wilderness journey the Lewis and Clark Expedition lost only one man—Sergeant Charles Floyd. And his August 20,1804, death came from a burst appendix, something that could have happened anywhere.

The first US soldier to die west of the Mississippi, the thirty-two-year-old Floyd was buried with full military honors on a bluff overlooking the Missouri River. Then the party moved on. Nearly a century later, a one-hundred-foot monument honoring the sergeant was built nearby and dedicated in 1901. The **Sergeant Floyd Monument** (2601 South Lewis Blvd.) stands on twenty-three acres maintained by the National Park Service.

The **Lewis and Clerk Interpretive Center** (900 Larsen Park Rd.; 712-224-5242) focuses on the time the Corps of Discovery spent in the area that would become Sioux Falls.

The **Sergeant Floyd River Museum and Welcome Center** (1000 Larsen Park Rd.) is housed in a former US Army Corps of Engineers work boat, the *M.V. Sergeant Floyd*. Commissioned in 1932, and named in honor of the sergeant, the 138-foot vessel plied the Mississippi until 1975. Sioux City bought the boat as surplus government property in 1993 and converted it to its present use.

By the early twentieth century, Sioux City was the tenth-largest railroad hub in the US. One of six railroads serving the city, the Chicago, Milwaukee, St. Paul, and Pacific had a thirty-stall roundhouse and assorted other shops for the maintenance and repair of steam locomotives and rail cars. In the early 1950s, the steam era ended, much of the facility was torn down with only half the roundhouse (containing six stalls) left standing. One of only seven roundhouses remaining in the nation, the complex of rail-related structures known as the **Milwaukee Road Shops Historic District** is listed on the National Register of Historic Places. The **Sioux City Railroad Museum** (3400 Sioux River Rd.; 712-233-6996) now occupies the property.

TAMA (TAMA COUNTY)

Tama County was organized in 1853 and the town of Tama was platted in 1862 when the Cedar Rapids and Missouri River Railroad cut through eastern Iowa.

Five years after Tama's founding, William Henry Neville Logan and his wife Eliza Jane settled nearby in 1867. A son they named Harvey Alexander Logan was born to the couple the same year. While that is supported by the 1870 US Census, the month and day of Harvey's birth has never been determined by researchers.

About all that is known of Harvey's early years in Iowa is that he had four brothers and a sister. After her husband died (or, by some accounts, disappeared), Eliza moved with her children to Gentry County, Missouri, in 1872 when Harvey would have been about five or six. This snippet of genealogical information would be of little interest to anyone but Logan family descendants except for what young Harvey grew up to be—a livestock thief, a train robber, and a killer who came to be known as Kid Curry. Even that might not have assured his place in history if he had not fallen in with one of the Wild West's most notorious outlaw gangs, the Wild Bunch.

Unlike some places that have tried to capitalize on their status as the birthplace of an infamous outlaw, Tama County has not put up a historical marker to note Harvey Alexander "Kid Curry" Logan's local roots. There are, however, two government buildings dating to the time of the Logan family's presence in Iowa. In nearby Toledo, the county seat, the **Tama County Historical Society & Genealogical Library** (200 North Broadway; 641-484-6767) is located in the old county jail, a two-story brick structure constructed in 1870. The museum includes a restored log cabin built the same year by a pioneer Czech family. Nearby is the Tama County Courthouse, a two-story brick and stone structure built in 1866.

WINTERSET (MADISON COUNTY)

The May 30, 1907, edition of the *Winterset Madisonian* reported the birth four days earlier of Marion Robert (soon changed to Michael) Morrison. Clyde and Mary "Molly" Morrison's son weighed in at thirteen pounds and was born at home in their modest, four-room frame house at 224 South 2nd Street. The Morrisons moved to California in 1914, where after high school in Glendale, Morrison enrolled in 1925 at the University of Southern California on a football scholarship. A bodysurfing injury cost him his scholarship and left him jobless, but all was not lost. As a favor to coach Howard Jones, who had given Western actor Tom Mix free game tickets, Mix got Morrison a job as a prop boy with Fox Film Corporation. There he met and was mentored by director John Ford, who gave him some bit parts. When Fox cast him for his first starring role in the 1930 movie *The Big Trail*, studio executives felt he needed a distinctive screen name and decided on John Wayne.

A seven-foot **bronze statue of Wayne** has stood near the restored home since 2010. Five years after that piece of public art's dedication, the **John Wayne Birthplace and Museum** (205 South John Wayne Dr.; 877-462-1044), a 6,100-square-foot museum focusing on the life and career of Winterset's most famous son, opened.

The Duke and Wyatt Earp

While it is true that legendary screen director John Ford had a brief acquaintance with Wyatt Earp before the old shootist died in 1929, and while it is also true that actor John Wayne was a protege of Ford, it is only legend that a young Wayne met Earp and heard some of his Old West stories. It also is only a legend that Wayne was one of Earp's pallbearers, though movie star Tom Mix and Ford were. But it *is* true that either based on what Ford told Wayne about Earp, or what Wayne later read about Earp, the Earp mystique did influence Wayne's portrayal of Western characters.

MINNESOTA

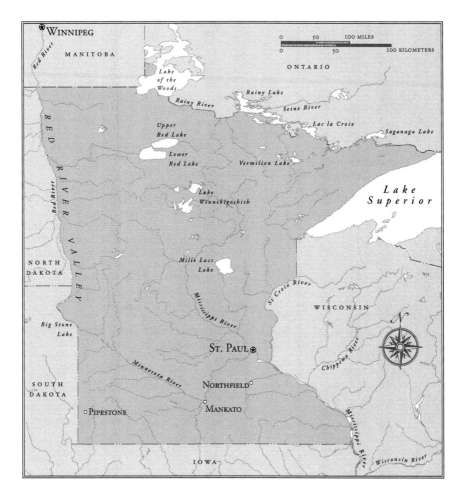

Acton (Meeker County)

Peter Ritchie moved his family to the fertile Minnesota River valley from Acton, a community in Ontario, in 1857. Joining him was the family of Robinson Jones and a handful of others, the men having decided to immigrate to the US after meeting the previous winter at a lumber camp on the upper Mississippi River. When a post office was established to serve the new farming settlement, it was named for the Canadian town they'd left behind. Acton remains a small farming community, but what took place there five years after its founding would have a profoundly tragic effect on the history of the West.

The Acton Incident

The triggering event of the nearly thirty-year war between the US and the Northern Plains Indians started with an argument on the part of four youthful Eastern Dakota (Sioux) hunters over whether to steal eggs from a farmer's henhouse. Still, that's something of an oversimplification. By the early 1860s, as the number of Euro-American settlers in Minnesota had grown to more than 150,000, the people who had lived there for generations had been forced to give up most of their land and move to a pair of reservations along the Minnesota River. Resentment of the federal government's efforts to assimilate them into the rapidly expanding dominant culture had built to a dangerous level. On top of everything else, due to government ineptitude and outright corruption on the part of some, the Dakota were suffering from hunger.

On August 17, 1862, four young Dakota men, on their way back to their village following an unsuccessful hunt, found an egg-filled nest at a settler's farm and debated whether to take them for their hungry people. One of the young men, opposed to the appropriation, was goaded by the others into confronting the settler, Robinson Jones, who owned the chickens. That devolved into the shooting deaths of Jones, his wife and daughter, and another couple at the hands of the four Dakota. When the hunters returned to their village and told tribal elders what they had done, another debate ensued. Was it time to take their land back from the whites or should amends be made? Those in favor of war prevailed.

In 1909, on the forty-seventh anniversary of the killing of the five settlers, the state placed a squat granite obelisk where the first blood had been shed. The five victims had been buried in a common grave at **Ness Cemetery** (24040 580th Ave., Litchfield). A large gray granite monument erected by the Meeker County Old Settlers Association in 1878 marks the grave. In 2012 the Meeker County Historical Society put two metal markers (53322 248th St., Grove City) adjacent to the 1909 monument to put the event and its aftermath into a more balanced perspective, or, as they put it, "to correct older language." Another modern marker (intersection of County Highway 23 and 550th Avenue), placed by the Meeker County Historical Society in 2021, summarizes the **Battle of Acton**, a clash that occurred the day after the killing of the five settlers.

FAIRBAULT (RICE COUNTY)

In most accounts of the so-called **Northfield Raid**, in which Jesse and Frank James, the Younger Brothers (Cole, Jim, and Bob), and others robbed the local bank on September 7, 1876, Northfield always gets the most attention. But Fairbault had a role in the aftermath of one of the Wild West's more famous crimes.

Following the robbery, as soon as a fast horse could cover the thirteen miles from Northfield to Fairbault, a rider handed Sheriff Ara Barton a note alerting him to the robbery and requesting that he be on the lookout for the perpetrators. The lawman rang the bell at the fire hall, which sent volunteer firemen and others running to see what was on fire. As soon as a crowd gathered, Barton read the note aloud and a posse quickly formed.

After the Youngers were taken into custody, they were locked up in the Rice County Jail and later that year faced trial in the Rice County Courthouse. Built in 1874, the ornate, two-story structure continued in use until destroyed by fire in 1931; the present courthouse stands on the spot (218 3rd St. Northwest).

Operated by the Rice County Historical Society, the **Rice County Museum** (1814 Northwest 2nd Ave.; 507-332-2121) has an exhibit on the Northfield Raid and Fairbault's part of the story.

Ara Barton continued to serve as sheriff until 1885. Following his death in Morristown, Minnesota, in 1898, he was buried in Fairbault's **Maple Lawn Cemetery** (Maple Lawn Avenue and Division Street West).

FORT RIDGELY (RENVILLE COUNTY)

In 1851, the Eastern Lakota ceded by treaty—under duress—millions of acres in southern and western Minnesota to the US government. The people then were settled on two reservations along the Minnesota River known as the Upper and Lower Sioux Agencies. Two years later, the US Army established Fort Ridgely just outside the Lower Agency. The government intended the garrison to act as peacekeepers as settlers by the thousands streamed into the newly available land. But in the summer of 1862, a variety of grievances on the part of the Dakota exploded into war.

In the twentieth century, Hollywood never seemed particularly interested in the 1862 conflict, but, while short-lived, it was one of the more extensive and bloody clashes with American Indians anywhere in the West. On August 20, some four hundred Dakota led by Little Crow attacked the fort, one of only a handful of instances anywhere in the Old West where Indians assaulted a US military post. Fighting for five hours, 280 soldiers and civilians fended off the warriors. Two days later, this time with eight hundred warriors, the Dakota attacked again. Cannon fire kept the warriors at bay until reinforcements arrived. As many as a hundred Dakota died in the battle.

Following the fort's abandonment in 1867, settlers cannibalized the buildings, leaving only the solidly built stone powder magazines and foundations. In the 1930s and early 1940s, archeologists excavated the ruins and the post commissary was rebuilt. The site became one of Minnesota's earliest state parks, but the Minnesota Historical Society took over management of the property in 1986. **Fort Ridgely** (72404 County Road 30, Fairfax; 507-628-5591) is seven miles south of Fairfax off State Highway 4. Four monuments placed by the state beginning in 1873 and continuing until 1914 stand at the site, in addition to twentieth-century historical markers.

Grand Portage (Cook County)

Grand Portage, on the north shore of Lake Superior inside the Grand Portage Ojibwe Indian Reservation, is one of the earliest places where west met east. For generations, a portage trail along a nearly nine-mile-long section of the Pigeon River not navigable by canoe facilitated the trading by the Ojibwe people of fur in exchange for European goods. The North West Company trading post remained active from 1731 until 1804.

Managed by the National Park Service since the 1950s, the 710-acre **Grand Portage National Monument** (170 Mile Creek Rd.; 218-475-0123) includes a replica of the log stockade that once protected traders, other reconstructed period structures, and an interpretive center.

Granite Falls (Chippewa and Yellow Medicine Counties)

Granite Falls was not settled until the early 1870s, but what would become Yellow Medicine County had earlier been chosen by the government as the location of the Upper Sioux Agency. Built in 1854, the complex was to serve as a distribution center for the annuity payments, goods, and food provided for by treaty in exchange for most of the Dakota people's land. In furtherance of the government's intention to assimilate the Dakota into white culture, the agency's other function was to provide education for Dakota children and instruction on farming techniques. At the onset of the 1862 Dakota War, tribal members looted and burned the agency. White traders and government employees were led from the agency eastward to safety by the Ampatutokicha, a Dakota also known as John Other Day. (Despite their treatment, the majority of the Dakota in Minnesota at the time had not been in favor of war.) In 1863 the government revoked the 1851 treaties, and the Dakota lost the remainder of their homeland. Following a period of internment at Fort Snelling, they were forced into Dakota Territory.

Opened in 1963, the **Upper Sioux Agency State Park** (5908 State Highway 67 East; 320-564-4777), eight miles southeast of Granite Falls, preserves the site of the reservation and has a visitor center that interprets the agency's history.

The **Yellow Medicine County Museum** (98 State Highway 67; 320-564-4479) has a large collection of American Indian artifacts and interpretive exhibits on the 1862 Dakota War among other displays related to the area's history and culture.

MADELIA (WATONWAN COUNTY)

Two weeks after the Northfield bank robbery, participants Charlie Pitts and the three Younger brothers—afoot and starving—approached a farmhouse near the Watonwan River about eight miles west of Madelia. While Ole Sorbel and his wife extended guarded hospitality to the men, the farmer's teenage son made a hard, fast ride to Madelia where he notified Watonwan County sheriff James Glispin that four of the Northfield raiders could be found at their place. The sheriff quickly organized a posse that found the suspects. The shootout that followed left Pitts dead and the Youngers all wounded.

The **Watonwan County Historical Center** (423 Dill Ave. Southwest; 507-642-3247) has an exhibit on the September 21, 1876, capture of the Youngers. A historical marker (Township Road 108, 0.3 mile from State Highway 3, on left when traveling south; GPS coordinates: N44° 03.69', W94° 34.16') near the scene of the shootout offers more details.

MANKATO (BLUE EARTH COUNTY)

At the confluence of the Minnesota and Blue Earth Rivers, Mankato was founded by Parsons King Johnson and others in the winter of 1852. The settlement was named for a Dakota chief whose village once stood at the site of the future community.

Here on December 26, 1862, in the largest public execution in the nation's history, US volunteer soldiers hanged thirty-eight Dakota men who had taken part in the uprising. And it could have been even more extensive. Originally, 303 Dakota had been condemned to hang for their role in the conflict, but President Abraham Lincoln pardoned all but thirty-eight believed to be the most directly involved in an attack on the German American settlement of New Ulm. The executed Dakota men were buried in a mass grave near the river.

In addition to those hanged, during the thirty-seven-day war, 77 US soldiers, 29 citizen-soldiers, 358 settlers, and 29 Dakota warriors were killed. The government closed the two reservations and forced more than three thousand Dakota people to vacate the state for new reservations in the Dakotas. (These numbers vary, but whatever the true count, the death toll was substantial.)

The **Blue Earth County Public Library** (100 East Main St.; 507-304-4001) stands at the site of the mass hanging. Outside the library is a historical plaque summarizing what transpired.

Across the street at **Reconciliation Park** is a twenty-foot-tall monument in the shape of a scroll listing the names of those who were hanged. Next to it is a six-foot-tall, two-ton limestone sculpture of a buffalo.

The Blue Earth County Historical Society maintains a county historical museum (606 South Broad St.; 507-345-4154) in the two-and-a-half-story mansion built in 1871 (and expanded in 1905) by Mankato businessman Rensselaer D. Hubbard.

MENDOTA (DAKOTA COUNTY)

In the language of the people who settled here first—the Dakota—
"mendota" means "the junction of one river with another." Founded
where the Minnesota River meets the Mississippi, Mendota is the
oldest town in southern Minnesota. The site of an eighteenth-century
French fur trading post, this is where US Army Lt. Zebulon Pike
signed the Sioux Treaty of 1805, the young nation's first treaty with
the Dakota people. Later, much broader in scope, another document,
known as the Treaty of Traverse des Sioux, was negotiated at Mendota
in 1851. Along with the Treaty of Mendota, also signed that year, this
agreement ceded almost all the Dakota land to the US government,
setting the stage for a bloody war that followed eleven years later.

Henry Hastings Sibley arrived here in 1834 as regional manager
of the American Fur Company, and in 1836 built a two-story stone
house that still stands. He went on to become Minnesota's first governor and would play a controversial role in the Dakota War of 1862
as commander of the Minnesota volunteer forces who suppressed the
uprising.

Mendota remained a small community, but it played a big part
in the development of the state. The history of the area is interpreted
at the **Sibley Historic Site** (1357 Sibley Memorial Hwy.; 651-452-
1596). The site includes four other historic structures associated with
the American Fur Company in addition to the Sibley House.

MORTON (RENVILLE COUNTY)

While Morton was not founded until 1882, the area's history goes
back much further. In 1853 a reservation known as the Lower Sioux
Agency was established about three miles south of the future location of Morton. Following the Dakota War of 1862, however, the
reservation—along with what was known as the Upper Sioux
Agency—was closed and the Dakota people were forced into the
Dakotas.

Birch Coulee Battlefield

A contingent of 160-plus soldiers under the command of Major Joseph R. Brown was dispatched from Fort Ridgely to bury the remains of settlers killed after the Dakota War broke out. On the evening of September 1, 1862, the soldiers made camp on open prairie near Birch Coulee Creek. That night, some two hundred Dakota warriors encircled the camp and attacked at dawn. During a siege that continued for almost thirty-six hours, the command lost thirteen soldiers and ninety horses. More than fifty of Brown's men suffered wounds, but only two Dakota men were killed. The troops were saved by the arrival on September 3 of reinforcements from Fort Ridgely.

The battle site (junction of Renville County Highways 2 and 18, off US 71, three miles north of Morton), managed by the Renville County Historical Society, offers a series of interpretive signs and monuments that tell the story of the battle.

Off State Highway 19, a half-mile northeast of Morton, stands a 52-foot gray granite monument erected in 1894 to honor those who died in the Battle of Birch Coulee.

Nearby stands the Loyal Indian Monument erected in 1899 to honor Ampatutokicha (John Other Day) and other Dakota figures who helped protect Minnesotans during the war.

The **Renville County Historical Society and Museum** (441 North Park Dr.; 507-697-6147) explores the history and culture of Morton and Renville County.

The **Lower Sioux Agency** (32469 Redwood County Highway 2; 507-697-6321) has a restored 1861 US government building and an interpretive center that explores the history and culture of the Dakota people. The site is owned and operated by the Lower Sioux Indian Community.

NEW ULM (BROWN COUNTY)

Settled by German immigrants in 1854, New Ulm saw the largest and bloodiest attack by American Indians against any town in the Old West. It came during the darkest days of the Civil War and exceeded many of that conflict's battles in its intensity. A small number of Dakota warriors attacked the town on August 19, 1862, but were repulsed. Still, five settlers died in the skirmish. Early on August 23, 1862, warriors under Mankato and two other headmen—twice unsuccessful in their recent attack on Fort Ridgely—swept in an arc-shaped wave from their cover in the woods toward New Ulm. Armed settlers behind barricades began firing on the charging warriors and succeeded in repelling them. But saving their town had come at a high price. Thirty-four of the defenders died and another sixty suffered wounds in the day-long battle. Fearing another assault following the attackers' withdrawal, the town's entire population fled on August 25 to other, more populated and better-defended, communities.

Housed in the old New Ulm post office, the **Brown County Historical Museum** (2 North Broadway; 507-233-2616) has three floors of exhibits, including displays devoted to the 1862 attack. The historical society's research library, Minnesota's third-largest archival collection, is maintained in the same building.

A monument in the median of Center Street (between State and Washington Streets) erected in 1891 by the state honors those who defended New Ulm during the Dakota War. Known as the *Defenders Monument*, it looks like it's made of stone, but artist Anton Gag fashioned it out of metal.

NORTHFIELD (RICE AND DAKOTA COUNTIES)

In the winter of 1855, John Wesley North left the Minnesota community of St. Anthony Falls to settle on land recently ceded by the Dakota people. North selected a site along the Cannon River because he believed it would be a good location for water-powered mills. It seemed thoroughly fitting that the townsite he had platted in 1856 should be called Northfield. The town became a center for wheat and corn growing, with several grain mills enjoying a brisk business, but twenty years after its founding, Northfield would become far better known for something else.

The Northfield Raid

Jesse James knew he and his colleagues in crime couldn't just barge into the bank with guns drawn, collect the cash, and ride off in a cloud of dust. Such an operation would take thorough planning, and that's what he and his confederates did. For days beforehand, they scoped out the countryside, collected local information, and cased their targeted financial institution.

Despite his previous criminal successes, and his careful preparation for this robbery, James miscalculated the resistance he and his men would encounter from the citizens of Northfield. He reasoned that a bunch of Yankee farmers wouldn't have many firearms and even further, they would lack resolve when faced by a band largely made up of hardened veterans of guerrilla warfare in Missouri.

At 2:00 p.m. on September 7, 1876, eight horsemen—all clad in linen dusters to conceal their handguns—cantered into town across the Cannon River bridge. Three of the men (James, his brother Frank, and Charlie Pitts) entered the bank, two men (Cole Younger and Clell Miller) waited outside, and the last three (Bob and Jim Younger and Bill Chadwell) sat their horses just across the bridge on Mill Square.

Inside the bank, acting cashier Joseph Lee Heywood (1837–1876) and two other employees proved less than cooperative, even at gunpoint. Heywood and the others played dumb and offered misinformation, mainly that the bank vault had a timer and could not be opened. That was false, but it cost the gang precious time. James drew his Bowie knife across Heywood's neck, not deep enough to kill, but enough to scare someone to death. When the thirty-nine-year-old bank employee yelled "Murder! Murder! Murder!" James knocked him senseless with the barrel of his six-shooter.

A townsman saw through the window what was happening inside the bank, and, as the late-nineteenth-century expression had it, "the ball began." Armed with shotguns and old rifles, several local men began firing on the robbers, who at first had shot only to create confusion and intimidation but now began to return fire in earnest.

When the wild battle ended seven minutes later, Clell Miller and Chadwell lay dead and all three Youngers had been wounded. Inside the bank, Heywood had been dispatched with a bullet to the head before the gunmen ran outside. Nicolaus Gustafson (1846–1876), a drunk Swede who had the misfortune of walking out of a saloon as one of the outlaws rode by, died four days later of a wound received from a stray bullet. (Another version of the story has one of the robbers, believed to have been Frank James, warning him to get back. But not understanding English, the emigrant did not comply, and James shot him.)

While the record is clear that two members of the James-Younger gang died in the botched robbery, it took generations before one of the dead outlaws was correctly identified as Chadwell. For years, accounts of the raid had his name as William Stiles.

It may have played out on the far eastern edge of the Wild West, but this shootout ranks right up there with Tombstone, Arizona's, 1881 OK Corral gunfight as one of the frontier era's most famous incidences of gun violence. Most historians agree the badly botched robbery was the beginning of the end of James's outlaw career.

The former First National Bank has been restored and is now the home of the **Northfield Historical Society's Bank Museum** (408 Division St.; 507-645-9268). A permanent exhibit includes the rifle that then-first-year medical student Henry Mason Wheeler (1854–1930) used to defend the town and the gold watch citizens presented him in appreciation. Wheeler, firing from the second floor of the Dampier House hotel (then in the 400 block of Division Street but no longer standing) was the citizen who killed Miller and wounded Bob Younger. Other artifacts connected to the raid are the saddle that came from Bob Younger's dead horse, two handguns, and a single spur.

Oddfellows Grove (Lincoln Street and Forest Avenue), a city park today, is believed by historians to be a remnant of the woods where the eight outlaws rendezvoused on the morning of the robbery. As they headed toward Northfield, the gang split into three groups to avoid looking suspicious. For the same reason, they had not carried rifles. But they all had revolvers.

In entering the town, the outlaws rode past the **Ames Mill** (319 South Water St.), which still stands. The significance of the site, however, goes beyond that. At the time of the robbery, the mill—which had a national reputation for quality—was owned by former Mississippi governor Adelbert Ames and Benjamin Butler. The James gang had somehow gotten word that the two men had deposited some $75,000 in the Northfield bank, the impetus for their decision to rob it.

The **Heywood House** (517 West 3rd St.), where the slain bank employee lived with his wife and daughter, and where his funeral was conducted following the raid, still stands at the corner of 3rd and Plum. The structure of the house is the same as when Heywood and his family occupied it, but its exterior has since been covered with stucco, and decks and a garage added. It is a private residence but can be viewed from the public right-of-way.

Both Northfield residents who died in the robbery, Heywood and Gustafson, are buried in **Northfield Cemetery** (1359–1399 Division Street). Heywood has a tall white marble monument; Gustafson lies beneath a more modern red granite headstone. Nearby stands a historical marker telling his story. Dr. Henry Mason Wheeler, who left Northfield in 1881 following the death of his first wife and their infant son, practiced medicine in Grand Forks, North Dakota, for most of the rest of his life. He died there as a respected member of the community but was returned to Northfield for burial in **Oaklawn Cemetery** (1415 Wall St.).

The **Northfield Area Chamber of Commerce and Tourism** (205 3rd St. West, Ste. B; 507-645-5604 or 800-658-2548) offers a brochure, "The Outlaw Trail," listing other sites in Northfield and the surrounding area with some connection to the raid. While Northfield gets a lot of visitors because of Jesse James, the town does not romanticize the outlaw and his cohorts. Instead, they honor those who stood up to the gang and remember the local lives lost that day. On the first weekend after Labor Day each year, Northfield celebrates **Defeat of Jesse James Days**. Over the course of the three-day event, the robbery-shootout is reenacted eight times.

PIPESTONE (PIPESTONE COUNTY)

Ceremonial pipe smoking was as much a part of Plains Indian culture as buffalo hunting. Tribe members lit pipes to make peace, to prepare for war, and as part of a number of other rituals. In addition, stone pipes were coveted trade items.

The pipes were made of what is known as pipestone, a reddish quartzite soft enough to carve but durable enough to hold burning tobacco. And for at least three millennia, the pipestone quarry, just north of the present town of Pipestone, has been one of the principal sources of the sacredly held stone. Pipes fashioned from stone quarried here have been found at archeological sites across the West.

Americans learned of the quarry from artist George Catlin, who visited the site in 1835. Initially, as Minnesota began to populate, American Indians did not object to Euro-Americans using the quarry. But the matter of access soon became a point of contention. The federal government established by treaty a one-square-mile reservation around the site in 1858 to assure tribal access, but by the 1860s, white settlers had for all practical purposes taken over the quarry and begun mass producing pipestone pipes to trade with reservation-bound American Indians. Not until the late 1920s, following a Supreme Court ruling, did American Indians receive monetary compensation for their loss. But the same ruling that provided payment to the Yankton Sioux held that the land around the quarry was federally owned. A decade later, however, American Indians regained full access to the pipestone quarry, which became a national monument in 1937.

The **Pipestone National Monument** (36 Reservation Ave.; 507-825-5464) now covers 301 acres and features a visitor center with interpretive exhibits. In addition to preserving the ancient quarry and educating thousands of visitors about this aspect of American Indian culture, the National Park Service oversees the guaranteed right of twenty-three enrolled tribes to continue their quarrying at the site.

The town of Pipestone was laid out in 1876 and incorporated in 1901. Two of its oldest and more striking structures, the 1888 **Calumet Hotel** (104 Main St.) and the 1899 **Pipestone County Courthouse** (416 Hiawatha Ave.; 507-690-7004), were built of locally quarried jasper quartzite.

The **Pipestone Museum** (113 South Hiawatha Ave.; 507-825-2563) focuses on the county's history.

RED WING (GOODHUE COUNTY)

A Mdewakanton Dakota headman named Tatanka Mani, known to early Euro-Americans as Red Wing, brought his people to this area around 1815. Their village, also called Red Wing, lay beneath Barn Bluff, a high prominence early French explorers had named La Grange ("the barn"). An 1851 treaty forced the American Indians from their land, but as a place name, Red Wing remained.

Settled in the 1850s, the town of Red Wing became a prosperous wheat farming center and riverboat landing. In 1889 the federal government opened a reservation near Red Wing for the Mdewakanton Sioux, now known as the Prairie Island Indian Community.

As a port, and later with rail connections, Red Wing flourished as an industrial center. Its prime industry, beginning in 1861 and continuing until 1967, was pottery. Over the years, eleven manufactures produced clay-based products that were widely distributed across the West.

Organized in 1869, the **Goodhue County Historical Society** (1166 Oak St.; 651-388-6024), is the oldest such organization in the state. The society operates a museum and maintains an archive of material related to the county's history.

The **Pottery Museum of Red Wing** (240 Harrison St.; 651-327-2220) has more than six thousand pieces of locally produced pottery, from butter churns to art objects.

St. Paul (Ramsey County)

The capital of Minnesota started out as Pig's Eye, for Pierre "Pig's Eye" Parrant's Pig's Eye Tavern. Being just about the only place a soldier from nearby Fort Snelling could enjoy a spiritous beverage, the Pig's Eye opened not long after the establishment of the fort and prospered. By the 1840s, the community that had grown up near the fort had become a busy Mississippi River steamboat landing and point of departure for travelers bound for western Minnesota or the Dakotas. One of those steamboats brought a French-Canadian priest who, in 1841, built a chapel he named for Paul the Apostle. Soon, Pig's Eye had a more dignified name, St. Paul. With the creation of Minnesota Territory, St. Paul was designated as capital. Located across from Minneapolis, St. Paul and its larger neighbor became known as the Twin Cities.

Visitors can begin their time here at the **St. Paul Visitor Center** (75 West 5th St.; 651-292-3225). For an overview of the state's history, visit the **Minnesota History Center** (345 West Kellogg Blvd.; 651-259-3000).

Fort Snelling

Standing on once-sacred Dakota Indian land where the Minnesota River meets the Mississippi (a point known in the Dakota language as "Bdote"), Fort Snelling was established in 1819 with construction beginning the following year. Originally named Fort St. Anthony, the post was renamed in 1824 after the officer who had overseen its construction, Col. Josiah Snelling. The garrison was abandoned in 1855 but reoccupied at the beginning of the Civil War. Troops from the fort took part in the 1862 Dakota War. Following the short and bloody conflict, Dakota families were held there until they were transported by boat to their reservation.

No matter its age and historic significance, for a time it looked like the old fort would be leveled so a freeway could cut through the former military reservation. Finally, after extensive debate, in 1960 the fort became a National Historic Landmark, Minnesota's first. Later, the fort was named a National Treasure site, the only one in the state. The state's top historic site, **Fort Snelling** (200 Tower Ave.; 612-726-1171) is managed by the Minnesota Historical Society. In addition to the restored buildings, there's a visitor center with interpretive exhibits and a documentary video. Living-history reenactors offer visitors a sense of what life at the fort was like during its heyday.

The post cemetery was established in 1870, but military burials at the fort dated back to 1820. In 1939 part of the military reservation was designated as a National Cemetery. Remains from nearly seven hundred graves at the old cemetery were exhumed and reburied in the new **Fort Snelling National Cemetery** (7601 34th Ave., South Minneapolis; 612-726-1127). More than 180,000 men and women who served in the nation's military are buried here.

The Empire Builder

When the primary mode of long-distance travel was rail, the fast, elite passenger trains that crisscrossed the West generally were named after things, from the Santa Fe Chief to the Sunset Limited. But the premier passenger train connecting Minnesota, North Dakota, Montana, Idaho, and Washington—the Empire Builder—was named after a person.

That individual was James Jerome Hill (1836–1916), founder of the Great Northern Railroad. Leaving his native Canada for the US, Hill started his transportation career working for a steamboat company in St. Paul. He began putting together his railroad in 1878 and proceeded to earn his Empire Builder nickname by opening the northern-most western states to the movement of people and goods. As its tracks moved westward, the railroad bought a vast amount of acreage from the federal government, developed townsites, and sold farmland to European immigrants and settlers from elsewhere in the US. Hill's influence on the development of the northern plains and Rockies was extensive.

The Great Northern is now part of the Burlington Northern Santa Fe Railroad, but the Amtrak train carrying passengers along the former Great Northern right-of-way is still called the Empire Builder.

Hill died in his St. Paul residence at the age of seventy-seven. He is buried in **Resurrection Cemetery** (2101 Lexington Ave. South, Mendota Heights).

Built by Empire Builder James Hill, the largest house in St. Paul is the 1891 **Hill House** (240 Summit Ave.; 651-297-2555). The house covers thirty-six thousand square feet and cost $931,000 to build, the equivalent of $28 million today. Built of red sandstone at the height of the Gilded Age, the three-story (plus basement and attic) mansion has forty-two rooms, thirteen bathrooms, twenty-two fireplaces, an eighty-eight-foot-long reception hall, and a two-story art gallery illuminated by skylights. A National Historic Landmark, the mansion became the property of the Minnesota Historical Society in 1978 and is open for tours.

ST. PETER (NICOLLET COUNTY)

First known as Rock Bend, this town was founded in 1853, platted in 1854, and renamed St. Peter in 1855. Two years later, territorial Governor Willis A. Gorman tried unsuccessfully to get the capital moved from St. Paul to St. Peter. The governor just happened to own the land on which he hoped the new statehouse would be built if the government moved to St. Peter. Legislative opponents kept that from happening.

Just north of St. Peter is a historic crossing of the Minnesota River known as Traverse des Sioux, which translates to "crossing place of the

Sioux," once a substantial Dakota village and French fur trading post. The Dakota called it Oiyuwege, "the place of crossing." Here, in 1851, one of the two treaties ceding most of the Dakota people's land, some twenty-four million acres, to the US government was negotiated. The pact, which the government never fully honored, set the stage for the bloody Dakota War of 1862.

The background of the two treaties and their significance is the focus of the **Treaty Site History Center** (1851 North Minnesota Ave.; 507-934-2160).

The site of the crossing is preserved as **Traverse des Sioux Park** (one mile north of St. Peter off US 169 on Traverse des Sioux Road).

SLEEPY EYE (BROWN COUNTY)

One of the West's more evocative place names honors Chief Sleepy Eye, a well thought of Sioux headman who had droopy eyelids. He was one of eight American Indians selected in 1824 to meet President James Monroe in Washington. As a Minnesota Historical Society marker near his grave later put it, "His fame was achieved not as a warrior or hunter but as a friend to explorers, traders, missionaries, and government officials." An advocate of peace, the chief signed four treaties with the US, including the **Treaty of Traverse des Sioux**, which conveyed to the federal government all Sioux land along the upper Minnesota River excepting a ten-mile-wide easement on both sides.

The chief and his people later settled in the area near the body of water that became known as Sleepy Eye Lake. The town of Sleepy Eye was laid out in 1872 and incorporated in 1903.

Chief Sleepy Eye died in 1860 while on a hunt in Roberts County, South Dakota. His grave in that state was located in 1898, and four years later his remains were removed to the Minnesota town that bears his name. A towering granite monument stands at his grave site (100 Oak St. North). At its base is this inscription:

Ish-Tak-Ha-Ba
"Sleepy Eye"
Always
A Friend of the Whites
Died 1860

The chief was further honored in 1994 with the dedication of an eight-foot-tall bronze statue in Wooldrik Park, adjacent to his burial place.

The **Sleepy Eye Depot Museum** (100 Oak St. North; 507-794-5053) is operated by the Sleepy Eye Historical Society and focuses on local history and the writer whose work gave the town a degree of national recognition—Laura Ingalls Wilder. The town of Sleepy Eye was frequently mentioned in the television series based on Wilder's most famous novel, *Little House on the Prairie*.

STILLWATER (WASHINGTON COUNTY)

Stillwater runs deep in the history of Minnesota. In fact, it's essentially the birthplace of the state.

In 1848 the first territorial convention that met to set up a territorial government took place at Main and Myrtle Streets. When the city was incorporated in 1854, well before Minneapolis, it was the largest in the state. Beyond its seminal role in the development of the state, Stillwater was a major lumbering center served first by steamboats and later by a rail connection.

The **Stillwater Commercial Historic District** covers eleven blocks and includes sixty-three vintage structures. In addition, the community has twenty-one buildings listed on the National Historic Register, and more than a hundred locally recognized heirloom homes and landmark sites.

As Governor Alexander Ramsey worked to develop a governmental infrastructure for the new territory, in 1849 he recommended to the legislature the creation of a "proper and safe place for confinement" for convicted persons. In other words, a prison. Territorial lawmakers agreed and appropriated $20,000 for such a facility.

A ravine on the north end of town known as Battle Hollow because of a fight that occurred there in 1839 between the Ojibwe and Sioux was chosen as the site for the **Minnesota Territorial Prison**. Construction began in 1851 and within two years, a three-story building with six cells and two areas for solitary confinement had been completed. The new prison also included a two-story residence for the warden.

The most famous inmates who did time at the prison were the Younger Brothers—Cole, Jim, and Bob—who soon after their arrest pleaded guilty to first-degree murder and received life sentences for their participation in the Jesse James–led Northfield Raid (see Northfield). The Youngers entered the prison in 1876 and were placed in adjoining cells. Bob died of tuberculosis in 1889. The two brothers, despite their reputation, were model prisoners. Cole's first prison job was in a shop making galvanized metal tubs, but he soon took on duties that required more thought than brawn, including working in the prison library, starting a prison newspaper, and eventually, as a nurse in the prison hospital.

Cole and Jim received a gubernatorial pardon in 1901. Reporters descended on them when they walked out in new suits carrying canvas grips (valises) given to them by the state. One journalist, intent on a "my how things have changed" story, took them into a store downtown and pointed to a telephone, bragging that he could talk to his newspaper in St. Paul over it. Soon a gasoline-powered vehicle chugged past, leading Cole to remark that pulling it with a horse would be safer. After a quarter century behind bars, the brothers found the world was different. Cole adapted to it. His brother did not, dying by suicide a year later.

The prison closed in 1914 when a new state prison opened in Bayport, but some of the buildings used for inmate labor programs continued in use into the 1970s. The old warden's residence was conveyed to the Washington County Historical Society in 1941 and developed into a museum. Among its other holdings, the **Warden's House Museum** (602 North Main St.; 651-439-5956) displays a wooden box made as a souvenir by one of the Youngers while in stir. A historical monument erected at the site in 1998 tells the story of the prison and the Youngers.

WALKER (CASS COUNTY)

On October 5, 1898, as US Army and Naval forces simultaneously prosecuted a war with Spain on opposite sides of the world—Cuba and the Philippines—troops of the US Third Infantry made history of another kind in far northern Minnesota.

What became known as the Battle of Sugar Point began when soldiers sought to arrest Chippewa Indian headman Ojibwe Bugonaygeshig (called "Old Bug"). He had been charged with illegally selling alcohol, but tensions with the Indian Service had existed for some time over timber rights. Triggered by the accidental discharge of a soldier's rifle, the off-and-on, day-long fight—which pitted seventy-seven infantrymen against only nineteen Indians—left seven soldiers and four civilians dead while the Indians suffered no serious casualties. The Chippewa had won what proved to be the last battle of the Indian Wars.

News of the fight gave rise to fears of a general Indian uprising. More troops were dispatched to the area from Fort Snelling and the Minnesota National Guard was mobilized, but the panic proved short-lived.

Later, Private Oscar Burkard received the Congressional Medal of Honor for his role in the engagement, the last such medal awarded for action during the Indian Wars. Though largely forgotten, the battle sparked a chain of events that led to US Forest Service oversight of all national forest lands. In addition, land ceded to the US by the Chippewa became **Chippewa National Forest**.

A metal plaque atop a stone base overlooking **Leech Lake** at the Whipholt roadside parking area, thirteen miles east of Walker on State Highway 200, describes the battle.

Operated by the Cass County Historical Society, the **Cass County Museum** (201 Minnesota Ave. West; 218-547-7251) has an exhibit on the area's American Indian and military history. The battle site, listed on the National Register of Historic Places, features foundation remnants of the house around which the battle took place, along with still-visible rifle pits dug by the soldiers. Archeological work done at the site shows centuries of American Indian occupancy.

WALNUT GROVE (REDWOOD COUNTY)

Charles and Caroline Ingalls moved their family, including future best-selling Western writer Laura Ingalls Wilder, to the newly laid out town of Walnut Grove in February 1874. At first they lived in a dugout on the bank of Plum Creek, but eventually Charles built the family a house on the land he farmed.

The Ingalls remained in Walnut Grove, where Laura's only brother was born in 1875, until the late summer of 1876 when they moved to Iowa. Roughly a year later, the family returned to Walnut Grove and stayed until they moved to South Dakota in the spring of 1879. Though the Ingalls were gone for good this time, years later Laura would figuratively revisit Minnesota after she became a writer.

Wilder's 1937 novel, *On the Banks of Plum Creek*, was inspired by her time at Walnut Grove. Walnut Grove was the setting for the *Little House on the Prairie* television series, though it was shot in California, not Minnesota. The Ingallses' real little house on the prairie, at least the one in Walnut Grove, no longer stands but the **Ingalls Dugout Site** (13501 CR 5) remains.

One and a half miles north of the site is the **Laura Ingalls Wilder Museum** (330 8th St.; 507-859-2358), which offers exhibits on the author's life.

INDEX

ABOUT THE AUTHOR

An elected member of the Texas Institute of Letters, **Mike Cox** is the author of more than thirty-five nonfiction books. Over an award-winning freelance career dating back to his high school days, he has written hundreds of newspaper articles and columns, magazine stories, and essays for a wide variety of regional and national publications. When not writing, he spends as much time as he can traveling, fishing, hunting, and looking for new stories to tell. He lives in the Hill Country village of Wimberley, Texas. To learn more about the author and his work, visit www.mikecoxauthor.com.